THE JOURNEY

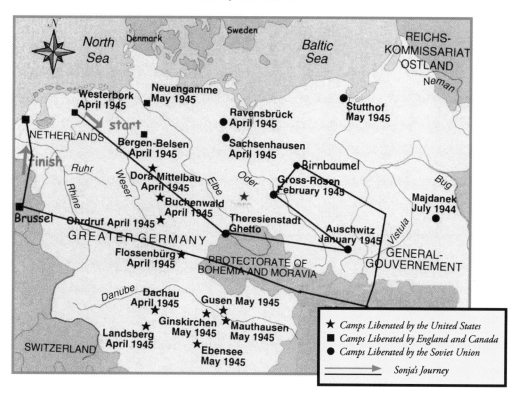

North Sea

Denmark

Sweden

Baltic Sea

REICHS-
KOMMISSARIAT
OSTLAND

Neman

Westerbork
April 1945

Neuengamme
May 1945

Stutthof
May 1945

start

NETHERLANDS

Bergen-Belsen
April 1945

Ravensbrück
April 1945

Sachsenhausen
April 1945

finish

Ruhr

Weser

Dora-Mittelbau
April 1945

Elbe

Oder

Birnbaumel

Gross-Rosen
February 1945

Bug

Rhine

Buchenwald
April 1945

Theresienstadt
Ghetto

Majdanek
July 1944

Brussel

Ohrdruf April 1945

GREATER GERMANY

Auschwitz
January 1945

Vistula

GENERAL-
GOUVERNEMENT

Flossenbürg
April 1945

PROTECTORATE OF
BOHEMIA AND MORAVIA

Danube

Dachau
April 1945

Gusen May 1945

Ginskirchen
May 1945

Mauthausen
May 1945

Landsberg
April 1945

SWITZERLAND

Ebensee
May 1945

★ Camps Liberated by the United States
■ Camps Liberated by England and Canada
● Camps Liberated by the Soviet Union

→ Sonja's Journey

And No More Sorrow

The World War II Memoirs of
Sonja Kiek Rosenstein Cohen

Cold Tree Press
Nashville, Tennessee

Originally Published in Holland (The Netherlands, 2006)

Published in the United States by Cold Tree Press
Nashville, Tennessee
www.coldtreepress.com

Printed in the United States of America
ISBN 978-1-58385-165-4

For my dear Mother, in memory of her loved ones

Acknowledgements

My whole life, especially these last five years, has revolved around the subject of World War II. Without the support of my family and friends I would have been unable to finish this book. I want to thank those who tolerated my 'nagging about the war.' It is over and done with. It's been 60 years. After putting pen to paper, after having finally written my mother's story, I hope that the therapy I experienced during my research will act as a catharsis and that I can pick up the pieces and continue where I left off five years ago.

Many thanks to Victoria Aarons, Dr. I. Berkovitz, Cisca Brier, Deborah Calla, Rubin Carson, Ezra van Coevorden, Nannette Cohen, Leny Cohen-Nijstad, Jack Hunter Cohen, Hans Colpa, Jennifer Cordey, J.M.A. Dané, Fenneke Dormits, Liz Franzeim, Gerrie Goudeketting, Marga Grunberg, Manfred Grunberg, Eric Guns, Uzi Hagai, Leah Haramati, Dennis and June Horner, Yankele & Tzwia Itzhaki, Jac. van der Kar, Mischa Kiek, Robert Kiek, Gerti Landau, Claus Lütterbeck, Judy Menco, René Mioch, Esther Nijenhuis, Leonie Oosterman, Yaron Pelzman, Jane Prosnit, Marianne van Praag, Max Rubenstein, Jules Schelvis, Mary Sheldon, Robin Sheldon, Linda Sherman, Neal Thompson, Ron Veeninga, Dave Walker, David Weinreb and last but not least Bram Benjamins, without whom this project would not have come to fruition.

Liliane Pelzman

Table of Contents

And No More Sorrow

The World War II Memoirs of
Sonja Kiek Rosenstein Cohen

The first couple of months nothing changed.
Even for us life was bearable.

When the summons arrived, I thought I am going on a trip,
I'll finally see something of the world besides Zandvoort and Den Bosch.

Mother, why are you crying?
Because, because… that's from before the war.

—Sonja Kiek-Rosenstein Cohen, Wassenaar, The Netherlands, 1999.

When the wicked, my
Enemies and my foes,
Came upon me to eat up my flesh,
They stumbled and fell.

—Psalm 27

Introduction

February 25, 2005 may seem like any other day, but it's not. Exactly 60 years ago today, on a Friday morning in 1944, my mother and her first husband Herman Rosenstein were shoved into a cattle car at concentration camp Westerbork in Holland and sent to Theresienstadt, a concentration camp in Czechoslovakia. They had been married eighteen months.

Until recently I resisted listening to my mother's stories about her journey, her war experiences and her concentration camp accounts. Whenever she brought up the subject of World War II, I would shut her out. As far back as I can remember I have tried to banish her stories from my consciousness. Horror stories, too excruciating for a child to comprehend, let alone to process.

I was born and raised in Holland and I knew early on that I had to leave there for my own sake. Looking back now, I understand that to survive emotionally I had to dispose of my mother's pain, the details of which I was to learn years later.

I was born in 1953 in Amsterdam in Holland, eight years after the end of World War II. The Dutch and particularly the Jews were still emotionally ravaged, as were my own Jewish parents. My mother came from a religious background. A traveling salesman, her father went to the synagogue every Saturday. Later, when he started his own business, he went daily. As a little girl, my mother would often accompany her father. She learned to read and pray fluently in Hebrew. After the war, in addition to losing her family, her first husband and most of her relatives, my mother also lost her faith. She did not have the strength to oppose her second husband, my father, Maurits Kiek, who did not want his children to be raised in the Jewish faith. Indeed, I had two brothers; neither was circumcised.

Maurits, a Jewish anti-nazi war-hero, attached to the British Intelligence Service, parachuted into occupied Holland and was captured by the Nazis. He was tortured and sentenced to death several times, yet he survived the war, albeit with a distorted personality that effectively blighted our lives.

Outside of our house, we never talked about or admitted to being Jewish. If someone asked what religion we were, I answered Protestant, as my father had told me to do. I realized early on that I was different from other kids. My Dutch classmates and friends had aunts and uncles, cousins and grandparents. I didn't. Mine had been murdered.

Anger and pain, the core bedrock of my parents' being, permeated everything. It was as standard as breakfast, lunch and dinner. As if by osmosis, my three siblings and I were imbued with my parents' emotional baggage. Consequently, we lived in continuous conflict with the world around us, with each other and most tragically within ourselves. A rather recent clinical term for such a psychological mind frame is "second generation syndrome." I am finding I am not alone. My heart goes out to all children who carry their parents' suffering, be it due to conflicts or war, human rights catastrophes or humanitarian emergencies. These children seldom enjoy a peaceful moment. Coming to understand my mother's trauma has made me sympathetic to trauma around me. Everybody has a story to tell. I decided to tell my mother's.

I have come to terms with the fact that her pain was instilled in me from birth. To deal with my pain, I must deal with my mother's pain first. To deal with the pain that comes with her story I need to know her story.

History doesn't happen in a vacuum. My mother's stories of her suffering led me to study the politics of Holland during World War II. This led me to the politics of Germany, which led me to Hitler, Himmler, Eichmann, Göring, Göbbels, Heydrich, Frank, Churchill, Stalin, etc. From there I moved on to study the history of concentration camps Westerbork, Theresienstadt and Auschwitz. Going further back took me to World War I and Napoleon. Back still further to the Spanish Inquisition when the Jews were expelled, tortured and even burnt alive if they refused to renounce their Faith. All of this and much more made me question my own Jewishness. I am Jewish but what does that really mean?

I realized that I knew nothing about Judaism. Was speaking Hebrew enough to make me a Jew? I started exploring what it meant to be Jewish, to be part of the above mentioned "second generation syndrome." I needed to understand what being Jewish in Holland in the 1940's implied. The more I thought about it, the more I wanted to understand what really happened. I became obsessed, entirely engrossed with my mother's past, like a tiger that won't let go of its prey. According to Dr. I. Berkovitz, my guide and mentor on this path, I became fixated.

Foremost, I must tell my mother's story because I don't want to forget it. I want to observe that today was the day of her deportation to Theresienstadt. I want to commemorate June 20, that fateful Sunday when, at the age of 21, she walked to work and got caught up in the middle of the last roundup in Amsterdam, thrown into an army truck and deported to camp Westerbork. The month of October I want to remember as the month she was deported to Auschwitz Birkenau and I want to celebrate every January 27, the day she was liberated.

Her experiences make me feel blessed and grateful for what I have; grateful for being born after the war, grateful for having known a period of relative peace in my part of the world, grateful for not having to go to bed hungry, grateful for living at the beach in California, grateful for not having to fear footsteps or banging on my door and people barking RAUS (Get out). I want to thank my mother for making me who I am. I often wonder whether it was her karma to suffer so that I might spend my life in liberty.

Reluctantly, I started giving in to my obsession, letting it lead me where it would. I started taping our conversations around 1998; I was in my forties, she in her seventies. Spending time together gave me insight into the woman I had called my mother, the woman whom I had loved but had needed to leave when I was barely sixteen. I got to know her, discovered what made her tick. She is an expert on classical music, her love for opera finally rubbed off on me, (as I am writing this I am listening to Puccini's *Tosca's Visi d'Arte*, one of her favorite arias). I discovered her sense of humor, her love for singing and her beautiful coloratura voice. Keeping notes and transcribing our conversations is how I got most of her story. I interviewed several of her friends who knew her from school, who had managed to escape and survive somehow. Thanks to those question and answer sessions, I have at long last gotten to know my mother and inadvertently myself.

—Liliane Pelzman
Santa Monica, California
2006

Home Turf

Noon. It is a warm summer day. Sonja Rosenstein sits at her desk typing intently on a bulky Remington typewriter. She reads back what she has typed. Preoccupied she rolls a strand of her very short hair around her index finger.

Outside she hears a car coming to a screeching halt. She startles and freezes. The familiar ominous footsteps fail to materialize. After a few moments she hears the car start up again and drive away. Shaken, she has a hard time concentrating on her work. She catches her image in a small mirror on her desk. Horrified she stares at her tightly cropped hair. She lets out a deep sigh. Her eyes wander along the stacked file cabinets that line the three walls. Most drawers are stuffed too full to close. Her eyes fix on a drawer labeled Cohen. Mother and Father, little Judie, Herman, all of them are gone, just like that. Everybody is dead, she thinks. Restlessly she looks at Perla Bierenhaak who sits working at a desk across from her. Perla feels Sonja's gaze and nods. "Go on. Just be back on time." Sonja jumps up. Swallowing several times, she manages to fight her tears. With a bang she pulls the front door shut behind her.

There are lots of soldiers about. There is rubble everywhere. Buildings are damaged. Streets are broken up. Store windows are shattered; some of them are boarded shut.

She jumps on her bike and hurries towards Amsterdam's main railway station, Central Station, all the while looking over her shoulder as if she's being followed. Out of breath she finds a spot to park her bike. Nervously she runs inside. It is swarming with people. Trains come and go. Family and friends welcome soldiers, slave laborers and civilians returning from the front.

She positions herself to the side, near a table with cups of coffee and a big sign saying FREE COFFEE. Close to tears she observes another group of arriving travelers, bald, thin and raggedy. Zombies with unseeing eyes. They move as if their souls have left their bodies a long time ago. Conspicuously they carry no suitcases. She understands their plight. A few weeks earlier she had arrived as part of a group just like it. Nervously she observes the spectacle. Every now and then a lucky traveler is welcomed and cries uninhibitedly of sheer joy. She quickly hurries along the length of the train to check if everyone has disembarked. Restlessly she glances at the huge station clock. The big hand jumps to twelve. Back at the office Perla nods supportively. Tomorrow is another day.

Desperately she rides her bike to the Plantage Franschelaan, number 17, where she's staying with her favorite Uncle Anton and his wife Aunt Jet. Anton is her mother's only sibling that has survived the nightmare. Anton Menco, a well-known doctor in Amsterdam and his wife, Jet, survived the hell of concentration camps Vught, Westerbork and Bergen Belsen. Anton got his wife and two kids back. Unabashed joy, impossible to describe in words.

Preoccupied Sonja opens the dilapidated wooden gate to the small front yard. Again the thought flashes through her mind that Father, Mother and little Judie are all gone. Vanished.

Awkwardly she pushes her bike into the tiny neglected front yard. As she places the bike against the scruffy hedge, it gives way almost causing her to lose her balance. It takes an effort not to crash with bike and all into the neighbor's garden. As she hastily tries to reposition the bike against the hedge, she remembers how well kept this yard had been three years earlier. Sometimes those three years seem like yesterday, other times like an eternity.

Her mind wanders back in time as she walks up to the front door. In that room over there she and Herman had discussed their wedding with Rabbi Sarlouis. Now it's Uncle Anton's consulting-room. Her parents had objected. Herman wasn't even allowed to visit her at home, let alone marry her. How could they let their daughter date a German refugee? They knew nothing about him. They couldn't verify anything he said. Thanks to Rabbi de Hond, she and Herman were eventually allowed to marry. Dear Rabbi de Hond! He and his wife, his daughters Lena and Esther and his son Mautje, are all dead. As if they never existed. Her family is also dead. But she isn't giving up. Not yet. She can't. Poor father, she thinks that day for the hundredth time. What will his horrible ending have been like for him? She gasps. Her parents never fought, that is to say she and little Judie had never witnessed even the smallest argument. Mother could be strict, sometimes angry but her irritation never lasted more than a minute.

Again there was no sign of Herman at the station today. How long can she keep this up, going to the station every day? Hoping against all odds. In her mind she has given up on her father, mother and little Judie, but Herman? Herman has got to return.

Just as she sticks her key into the lock the front door opens. A handsome man in uniform salutes her as he is leaving. Without paying attention she mumbles, "Excuse me." She doesn't notice that he keeps looking at her until she enters the house and shuts the front door. Then he gets into his car and drives away.

She leans against the inside of the front door and bursts out in tears. But how can they all be gone? She gets two index-size registration cards from her purse. Her eyes are fixed on the date in red pencil, 29-6-'43 and the word DEPORTED written over her father's name.

As she hangs her jacket on the coat stand, her cousin Judie approaches through the long hallway.

"Did you see my cousin?"

"Your cousin? What cousin?" She knows her cousins Aaron and Meijer are dead.

"He just left. Didn't you just see the guy in uniform leaving? That was Maurits Kiek. You know, my mother's nephew."

Without taking a breather Judie continues, "He was working for the British Intelligence Service and dropped in occupied territory, captured by the Germans and sentenced to death in Belgium. The Americans finally liberated him in Czechoslovakia."

"Oh, that was Maurits? I guess I did see him."

Judie notices the cards in Sonja's hand.

"What are those?"

"My parents' registration cards. I didn't want them filed among the cards of the people that are confirmed dead and not coming back."

Sobbing now, devastated, she continues, "I was in such a hurry, I forgot little Judie's card." Cousin Judie gives her a hug.

"Come on, take off your jacket. Have a cup of tea with us."

JACOB

Jacob Cohen was born on July 11, 1892 in the city of Leeuwarden, in the north of Holland. He was the eighth of ten children. His mother kept a kosher home. Jacob's father David wore a skullcap at home and a hat when he went out. He was known for being extremely generous. When Jacob was a kid, his father moved the family to Amsterdam. They settled on the Waterlooplein, the center of the Jewish neighborhood. In Amsterdam too, David became known as a giving man. Years later, during one of Sonja's school trips to the Neie *shul*, the teacher called her name.

"Yes, I am Sonja Cohen."

"Do you see that big silver dish? Your grandfather David gave that to this *shul*." She proudly reported the experience at home. (The word *shul* means school in Yiddish, a Jewish/German variation of the German language and the word synagogue are interchangeable because a synagogue is often a place of study).

HENRIETTA

Henrietta "Jet" Menco was born December 26, 1896 in the south of Holland, in the city of 's Hertogenbosch, (informally known as Den Bosch). She had three siblings, sister Wilhelmina or "Mientje" and two brothers, Anton and Maurits. Their mother Judikje lost her hearing at the age of thirty. The kids were used to shouting from early on. Henrietta's father, Hijman Salomon Menco bought and sold wholesale textile: yarn, fabric and scrap metal. The rags were sorted, ground, run through the spinning wheel, rewoven and finally made into pieces of fabric again. He carried out what we know today as "recycling."

They lived in a big three-bedroom house. That was a great luxury in those days. Next to the house was a huge shed with a sign on the roof towering high over all other roofs: H.S. MENCO RAGS AND METALS. The workers sorting the rags lived with their families in small houses adjacent to the shed.

When Henrietta and Jacob took their daughters to Den Bosch to visit her parents, the train crossed the river Waal at Zaltbommel. Sonja and little Judie would get up and excitedly search for the roof sign in the distance. Henrietta was proud that her daughters enjoyed seeing her name on the roof. Sometimes people thought Henrietta was "stuck up" because of her yelling, but yelling had become a habit due to her mother's condition. However, as they got to know her, they noticed she was actually rather shy.

When the time came, Maurits joined his father in the business while Anton had been accepted to study medicine in the city of Utrecht. After having graduated and having treated wounded soldiers during World War I, Anton started a medical practice in Amsterdam. Henrietta and Mientje were fascinated by the big city and moved in with their brother. Henrietta and Mientje welcomed the patients and kept the household going. These were exciting times. Anton started making a name for himself. His practice started to flourish.

One of Anton's patients is Jacob Cohen. He suddenly feels sick all the time. To meet Henrietta he thinks up one ailment after another. He has turned into a nice man with a sense of humor. He has joined an amateur acting group, he is tolerant and soft-spoken and he would later prove to be the most loving father in the world. Henrietta and Jacob have found each other.

At this time Jacob sells woolen and silk materials for a firm called Ter Veen and de Lange in Amsterdam. In time he plans to start his own business.

"Will she fit in?" Jacob's father asks him. "After all, her family is much better off? Is that going to be a problem? She comes across as aloof, almost arrogant."

"It may seem that way, but that's not at all what she's like. She is really shy," Jacob defends her.

"Have you promised to marry her?"

"Yes."

"Then marry her. You have our blessings."

February 1, 1922 they celebrate the wedding with lots of family and friends. They spend their honeymoon in Belgium. Jacob gives notice at his job in Amsterdam and starts working with Maurits in the wholesale business of his father-in-law, down in Den Bosch.

SONJA

November 21, 1922 Sara "Sonja" Wilhelmina Cohen is born at 6 am in Sint Carolus hospital in Den Bosch. She weighs six pounds. It's a difficult birth. Jacob says the *ha-gomel* prayer because Henrietta has survived the dangerous birth. Jacob misses Amsterdam and four years later he decides to move his family to Amsterdam. In 1926 their new address becomes Swammerdamstraat 6, a two-bedroom home with a garden and a long dark frightening hallway through which toddler Sonja often runs to fetch the paper from the mailbox. Lacking central heating, she catches pneumonia two or three times every winter. Uncle Anton, meanwhile, has married Henriette "Jet" Salomons.

April 1924. Hitler served nine months of a five-year prison sentence for a failed Munich putsch. He was released by Christmas of that same year. While confined to a hotel-like jail, he started working on Mein Kampf. Once released, he created the SS, a special bodyguard unit within the storm troopers. In 1929 he appointed Heinrich Himmler head of the SS.

Fascinated Sonja listens to the stork story. A stork has bitten her mother in her tummy and now there is a baby brother or sister in her tummy. That's why her mother needs to rest in bed. Sonja stays with Anton and Jet. Every day Jet walks Sonja home to visit her mother. When Anton buys a new car they drive, until Anton notices a scratch on the car. Then it's back to walking again. On her first visit Sonja, captivated by the stork story, runs into her mother's bedroom and searches under the blankets for the stork bite. Impatiently nurse Corrie pulls her away.

"There's nothing to see," her mother explains, "Corrie just wrapped the wound with a bandage."

Sonja's sister Judie is born on November 2, 1926. To distinguish between Sonja's sister Judie and Sonja's cousin Judie, her sister is called "little" Judie.

Back in Amsterdam Ter Veen rehires Jacob but the competition has become fierce. Jacob travels a lot. Living out of a suitcase and not having a union doesn't make his business any easier. He leaves early Monday morning and returns Friday before sunset. Every Monday morning he kisses Sonja and little Judie goodbye telling his wife affectionately, "Jetje, take good care of the girls." From the moment he leaves, Sonja and little Judie wait impatiently for his return. He often surprises them with a present.

During the dark winter months, school is out on Fridays at 3:30 p.m. Before rushing home, Sonja and Judie cheerfully head to the library to pick up a book. Mother has done her Friday food shopping and they know that a pickled meat and liver sandwich, a Dutch delicacy, is waiting for them. After updating their mother on their school stories and teachers' comments, they take a bath and put on their dressing gowns. The countdown to father's arrival has begun. Then that precious moment arrives. They are exuberant. Father is home. They talk a while before he gives Sonja and little Judie their present. Sonja gratefully unwraps a postcard from some actor or other she adores and Judie is delighted with some other knick-knack. Next Jacob takes a bath, shaves and goes to *shul*. While Jacob is in *shul*, Sonja prepares the table for the Sabbath. She stones the dates and fills them with Brazil nuts. She sets the table with a white tablecloth and silver cutlery. She covers the Challa bread with a special bread cloth that she embroidered at school. (Challa bread is plaited bread eaten on the Sabbath and festivals). She positions the crystal glasses precisely. Little Judie places the forks and knives. Then they wait for father to come home. Traffic dies down around sunset and peace and quiet blankets the neighborhood. Henrietta lights the candles and sets the earlier prepared dinner on the hotplate.

Jacob blesses his daughters before they start eating. At the table, as he cuts the bread, Sonja studies his hands. She knows their little fingers look alike and she lets no Friday dinner go by without commenting on it. He laughs, even blushes. She wants so much to look like her father. Henrietta teases him, saying that he had wanted a son, but he doesn't like that. Especially when Sonja says, "if I had been born a boy, we could have put on *tefillin* together. (*Tefillen* are two black leather boxes containing four biblical passages written by a scribe attached by leather strips to the left arm and upper forehead. See Deut. 6:8).

"Not so," he would say, "I am very pleased with you."

After dinner Sonja and little Judie help with the dishes; one dries while the other puts them away. Then it's time to sit down and read. Jacob reads the Torah, Henrietta a woman's magazine, Sonja and little Judie a library book.

Jacob and Henrietta are royalists; they respect and support the Royal family. For Sonja the saga of the Dutch royals is a fairy tale. She knows everything about them. Away on his trips, Jacob often sends Sonja a postcard of Princess Juliana and Queen Wilhelmina. She holds on to every single one of them—until the devastating day when she has to part from them.

Every year in the month of September Queen Wilhelmina and her daughter Princess Juliana stay at the Queen's palace in Amsterdam for eight days. Every year Sonja and her father line up devotedly along the crowded streets to welcome their arrival. As the royal carriage passes by, Jacob tips his hat and bows respectfully to the Queen. The mayor returns Jacob's greeting by doing the same. Sonja loves the spectacle of it all.

At the age of five she turns into a little performer, clowning about with lipsticks, imitating female opera singers. Jacob starts taking her to *shul*. She adores her father and loves every minute of it. Her mother having suffered childhood polio has trouble walking and stays home with little Judie.

Jacob is a *parnas* and has a front row seat in the usually packed synagogue. (*Parnas* is a supervisory position; honorary in nature.) Too small to see Rabbi de Hond, Jacob allows her to stand on the bench. The men standing nearby spoil her with pieces of licorice and chocolate. After the service on their way home and weather permitting, she and Jacob stroll through Artis, the Amsterdam zoo, and marvel at the Dutch bank building taking shape. Together they watch the Dutch flag high up on top of the building, waving in the wind. Every week Jacob notices its progress and mumbles, "Heavens, they are building fast." In the summer months when a violinist plays in the Utrechtsestraat, Jacob gives Sonja two cents to throw into the hat. He proudly picks her up and holds her as they listen together to the violinist. Returning home she runs to her mother and tickles her back for a dime.

Jacob moves his family to a bigger home on the third floor in the Andreas Bonnstraat 14. For a while they have a gorgeous view of Queen Emma hospital. They are doing well; they have a vacuum cleaner and a telephone. Regrettably they lose their view when a brewery company starts building a new office. She hears her father tell her mother, "Jet, I am starting my own business. It won't be long now before we move to a nice house in the south of Amsterdam." (Amsterdam-South is a pleasant, upscale, semi-suburban neighborhood in Amsterdam with many Jewish residents).

The 1930 census reported one hundred and ten thousand practicing Jews, twenty thousand of whom reported that their religion was not part of their daily life.

The story of *Sinterklaas* goes that every year on December 5th, *Sinterklaas* shows up in Holland on horseback from Spain with Piet, his black helper. Sint rides on his white horse over rooftops, while Piet keeps up with him on foot. Piet climbs down chimneys to leave presents for the good children. Piet takes the naughty children back with him in a rucksack to Spain. To get on Sint's good side, children leave water and a carrot for Sint's horse. Sint has a long white beard and resembles Santa Claus.

Conforming to the annual Sinterklaas tradition, Sonja prepares a bowl of water and a carrot for Sint's horse. When she accidentally spills some water and makes matters worse by eating half the carrot, her mother remarks the following morning wryly, "Sint made a real mess of it this time." When Sint actually appears (in schools, in stores, at *Sinterklaas* parties) and asks Sonja if she has been a good girl, she answers matter-of-factly "Of course I have," but he sees her short bitten nails and is not convinced, "If you haven't stopped biting your nails next year, Piet and I will be taking you back to Spain with us." Terrified she never bites another nail.

Every year, at the beginning of summer, Henrietta cashes stocks her father gives her and uses the money to take her daughters to Zandvoort, a holiday resort on the North Sea, eight miles west of Amsterdam. Every year on July 31, a cab comes to pick them up and their hamper filled with clean clothes. Jacob joins them on the weekends. Every summer they stay four weeks at hotel

Hiegentlich, they rent the same room and they eat at the same table in the same dining room. Excited they get up at seven thirty, have breakfast at eight thirty and by nine o'clock they start the ten-minute walk to the beach concession where Henrietta rents a cabana with its green beach chairs across from the town's casino. For the entire four weeks a sign above their beach chairs reads, "Henrietta Cohen." From the pavilion Sonja walks to the library across from the train station and returns with six books at a time. Now and then she meets friends from school. One Saturday morning she meets Toni on the beach.

"What are you doing here? You're not supposed to walk on sand. Leaving footprints in the sand is like writing. You're not allowed to write on the Sabbath."

Afraid of having done something wrong, she tells her father.

He calms her down.

"You may tell her that I said it's okay with me."

It is in hotel Hiegentlich where they meet Helène and Abraham Gans. They own a green Ford and have a private chauffeur. Originally from Hamburg, where they owned realty, Mr. and Mrs. Gans have come to Holland to evade Hitler. In Holland, Mr. Gans switched to the fur business. They have two sons. Son Hansfried is at boarding school in England and spends the summer months with his parents in Holland. Sonja and Hansfried become friends. Back in Amsterdam, after their summer vacation, Sonja often finds a letter from Hansfried waiting under her dinner plate. Helène and Henrietta both hope to see the day their children fall in love.

Every Thursday Sonja and her sister go to City Hall to watch couples get married. Thursday's ceremonies are free of charge and lots of couples take advantage of that. At home, everything is cleaned and spotless for the Friday. She and little Judie are thrilled for father is coming home tomorrow.

From 1930 to 1936 Jacob is a member of the board on Sonja's primary school, the Herman Elte School. She is the class clown. She has everybody in stitches. She reads fairy-tales, giving each character a distinct voice. The king gets a deep raspy voice; the gnomes speak with high-pitched voices. At the end of the hour when the bell rings, no one moves until Sonja has finished reading. They have Torah, the First Testament, class every day. When they discuss the word *parnas*, she raises her finger eagerly.

"Little Sonja Cohen," says master Stibbe, with his permanent runny nose. "Why don't you tell us?"

Dramatically she asks if it means, "taking care of." He pats her hair.

"Why would you say that?"

"My father," she says proudly, "is a *parnas* in the Neije *shul*. He takes care of problems."

Jacob beams when he hears the story.

In 1932 Jacob buys a radio for the living room. Programs are distributed by wire, a precursor of today's cable radio. There are three channels. Before starting her homework, she solemnly turns the radio on to the opera channel and organizes her books by subject. As she starts studying her mother enters the room and promptly switches the radio off.

"You can't study with the radio on."

Sonja disagrees and as soon as her mother leaves the room she switches the radio back on and listens to Liliane Harvey, Willi Fritsch, Jeanette MacDonald, Amelita Galli-Curci, Jan Kiepura and her all time favorite Martha Eggerth. Soon enough she discovers acting. She is good at it too.

January 1933 Hitler became Reich's Chancellor of Germany. Scores were settled. Opponents disappeared into concentration camp Dachau. The Nazi party flag, a black swastika on a red background, flew alongside Germany's national flag. April 1933, a national boycott against Jewish businesses began.

Depending on the weather, they go for tea at Jet and Anton's. Anton's medical practice is flourishing. Every year in March, Jet throws a party to celebrate her combined birthday and wedding anniversary. The entire family turns up. Sonja and cousin Judie play queen and lady-in-waiting. A fancy dress from Jet's closet serves as a veil. Sonja has to be the queen. Judie doesn't protest and stands obediently behind her on the bedroom balcony as Sonja royally greets the pedestrians on the sidewalk below. The most exciting moment arrives when Jet tells Sonja to pick out a piece of clothing Judie has grown out of. Bored with her own clothes, Sonja is beside herself with joy.

March 1935. The Nazis instructed a young blond girl to speak over the wireless radio in a friendly manner to the listening audience. "Attention, attention, here is radio Paul Nipkow. We greet all you listeners in the Berlin region with 'Heil Hitler.'" In the studio she gave the Hitler salute.

In 1936, while walking home from school, Sonja sees a crowd gathered at a cigar store. They are reading a public announcement. Curious, she works her way through the crowd to the front and reads that Crown Princess Juliana is engaged to marry Bernhard von Lippe-Biesterfeld. Sonja is euphoric and runs home. Out of breath she tells her mother the good news.

To introduce the future prince to the people of Holland, the royal couple travels through the whole country and of course they visit Amsterdam, the capital of Holland. Most schools get to perform something. The Jewish schools unite for the event and rehearse with legendary S. H. Englander. Sonja is elated. She is going to be singing for the queen.

When the day arrives the whole Jewish community is present. The Meijerplein is a sea of waving miniature flags. With the crowd screaming in the background, first the mounted police go by, followed by the chief of police and the mayor. Finally the carriage with Queen Wilhelmina, her daughter Juliana and fiancé prince Bernard pass by. The square is packed with people moving in unison. The red carpet is spotless. The doors of the *shul* are open. The candles in the chandeliers are lit; the doors to the Holy Ark are open. The carriage stops in front of the entrance. The children gather around the carriage and sing as if their lives depend on it. A moment she will never forget.

March 1936. Hitler spoke in Karlsruhe. "Germany has no intentions of entering Poland, Belgium, Czechoslovakia, and France." (J.C. van Zeggelaar, Five years Nazi-press)

In 1936 Sonja goes to a Jewish high school. According to Jewish tradition, she is off on Saturdays and goes to school on Sundays. History, music, singing and acting are her favorite subjects. An aspiring actress, she draws attention to herself by making fun of the teachers. She glibly asks funny questions. Her classmates laugh themselves silly, except for the new ones, the ones that have fled Hitler Germany and have not yet adjusted to their new lives in neighboring Holland. One of these new students will change the course of her life.

Herman Rosenstein is a German refugee. With his handsome athletic looks, blue eyes, fair-hair and German accent, she finds his boyish charm irresistible. She loves it when he talks to her in German. Classmates snicker (she doesn't) when the teacher enters the classroom and Herman jumps up with typical Prussian military discipline. She reminds him affectionately that he's in Holland now, he can stay seated, but he remains standing next to his desk until the teacher nods at him to sit down. She is 14 years old, exactly one day his junior and totally in love. They start spending time together.

HERMAN

Herman is born November 20, 1922 in Lübeck, Germany. He is believed to be the product of a one-night stand between his Jewish mother Irma Lissauer and a handsome blue-eyed blond-haired Aryan soldier whose name she didn't quite catch. Irma notices that her son is a carbon copy of his anonymous dad. Wanting to restore her reputation after Herman's birth, Irma marries Chaim Rosenstein. Rosenstein lawfully adopts Herman and Herman Lissauer is now called Herman Rosenstein. He grows into a handsome and athletic young man. He does well in school and Irma and Chaim are proud of him. He is popular and not lacking for friends. One day, while in the shower after a physical education class, two new classmates tease him for being circumcised. He starts asking questions at home. Why is he circumcised? How come he's blond with two dark Jewish parents? Irma decides to send Herman to her sister Bettie, in Holland, not only because of his relentless probing about his biological father, but also because Hitler's Germany is becoming too dangerous. Bettie Emmering and her two children, Jennie and Alphons, live in Amsterdam, Swammerdamstraat 44, and a few doors down from Sonja. Alphons has recently married and moved out, so Herman gets his room.

For the nine o'clock classes they have to be at school by quarter to nine. It's a fifteen-minute walk for Sonja. She usually leaves at 8:30; this gives her plenty of time. Suddenly she wants to leave at 8 o'clock.

"Why do you want to leave so early?" Her mother knows Herman is waiting. She has met him and is not impressed. She has decided he is far too young for her daughter. Besides, he is a refugee and they know nothing about him.

"Finish your breakfast," her mother orders sternly. Barely swallowing her last bite she runs out the door to meet Herman. After school Herman walks her home. To avoid being seen by her mother, they say goodbye behind a nearby wall. She loves their moments together. What a shame they have to sneak around like that! Her girlfriends are allowed to bring their boyfriends home. Why isn't she? It's not fair. Her father seems to understand her better. He is more supportive, more sympathetic.

When Herman walks her to Jet and Anton's, he drops her off unseen. She rings the bell. One of Jet's nephews opens the front door; Maurits Kiek, 29 years old, pinches her cheek.

"Who are you?"

"I am Sonja."

"Sonja who?"

"Sonja from Uncle Anton's sister Henrietta."

"Ah, you have become a big girl."

Still thinking of Herman, she half smiles and enters the house. On days like that, when they all get together they laugh a lot. With a piece of cake and a cup of tea, it's time to crack jokes.

At one of such get-togethers, Sonja notices everyone is wearing a garment previously owned by another relative. They go down the line and try to remember who is wearing what from whom. Uncle Anton, Aunt Jet, Uncle Maurits, Aunt Esther, Aunt Sol, Aunt Trees, Henrietta, Sonja, little Judie, cousins Judie and Hans. They laugh so hard that their bellies hurt. Before leaving she grabs a handful of chocolate for Herman, who is waiting for her around the corner.

"You better invite him in," Aunt Esther advises Henrietta, "Inside they're up to less mischief than outside."

Finally Herman is allowed to call on Sonja at home. Again her mother is not impressed.

"Where are you two going?"

"We are meeting Emile. Gerdi is playing basketball." Gerdi plays on the school team. Herman and Emile, Gerdi's boyfriend, want to be supportive and often go to see Gerdi play. Sonja joins them when she can. On Sundays Sonja and Herman meet at Gerdi's. If Gerdi's parents are home, they visit Herman's married cousin Alphons instead. They make out, although afraid of the potential consequences.

Gerdi's parents and those of Emile are refugees from Poland, from a small unknown village called Oswiecim, later known as infamous Auschwitz.

1937. American automobile manufacturer Henry Ford received the Cross of the German Eagle Order from Hitler.

1938. Austrian Germans welcomed Hitler's occupation of Austria with flowers and Nazi flags. Thousands of German Jews fled to England, France, North and South America and Palestine. Many fled legally, others illegally into neighboring Holland, hoping to find work, to start a new business or in any case a new life. Since Holland had been neutral in World War I, these refugees hoped Holland would be safe this time as well, but as Holland was in the middle of a major recession, the authorities refused to issue work permits. (Was the Dutch government strictly neutral during the 1914-1918 war? They let the German army on their way to Belgium pass through the province of Limburg in 1914. Were the Dutch unable to resist the mighty and most powerful army in Europe?)

The German refugees that did make it to Amsterdam established a German club. The German club was mainly a vehicle to keep unemployed refugees and their kids off the streets and out of trouble. The club provided history and art classes and Dutch language classes. It organized social and cultural events. Sports and camping trips were very popular. On Sundays members got together while coffee was served. For fear of jeopardizing their delicate relationship with Nazi Germany, the Dutch government demanded that German Jews stay out of politics. Discussing politics therefore was off limits at the club. Most group leaders stuck to this rule. German Jews didn't mix well with their Dutch counterparts. They thought the latter were less educated and less wealthy.

Herman, now sixteen years old, switches to a technical college where he studies automotive mechanics. This gives him a chance to study and make money at the same time. He visits the German Club every day. He plays table tennis with his buddy Manfred and quickly becomes known as an ace player. The girls at the club like his striking smart looks. He is generous, honest and kind. The combination of his blue eyes and blond hair make him look German, not Jewish at all. He is discrete and refuses to discuss Sonja with the probing Manfred.

The Committee for Jewish Refugees offers Herman a job. CJR is part of the Committee for Special Jewish Interests and operates as an intermediary between the Dutch government and the Jewish refugees. Founded in 1933 to assist refugees from Nazi Germany, CJR helps obtain immigration papers, assists with housing accommodation, work permits, financial matters, etc. In charge of CJR is Dr. Sluzker, a Jewish lawyer from Vienna who offers Herman a position as his assistant. Herman gladly accepts. He celebrates his good fortune at the German club with Sonja, Gerdi, Emile, Manfred, Manfred's sister Marga and a few other German friends. Herman works hard and Sluzker is satisfied. Sonja and Herman spend a lot of time together and with Gerdi and Emile.

1937

Jacob starts his own business. He only travels locally. Bolts of cloth, mostly silk and wool, are piled up in the spare bedroom. Every morning after a light breakfast, before visiting his customers, he goes to *shul*. He likes having his own business and he is optimistic about the future. On Saturdays Sonja, now fifteen years old, meets her father at ten o'clock in *shul*. After the service they walk home together. Jacob proudly notices that his little girl is blossoming into a beautiful young woman. She knows she has a pretty face, but her arms and legs could have been longer. Bigger breasts would have been fine too. Quietly singing an aria by his side, he radiates as they walk home together.

1938

Dutch border guards were instructed to stop all refugees from entering Holland. They handed all German Jews, trying to cross into Holland, back to Nazi Germany. Once in the hands of the Gestapo, Geheime Staats Polizei or Secret State Police, they were taken to concentration camps where they were killed. Many Jews committed suicide.

Herschel Grynzpan, a Jewish young man living in Paris, angry with the Nazis for mistreating his family in Germany, murdered a German diplomat. In retaliation for the diplomat's murder, Nazi propaganda minister Josef Göbbels sanctioned 'Kristallnacht,' in English also known as the "Night of the Broken Glass." Göbbels ordered all synagogues and Jewish-owned stores in Germany and Austria destroyed. In fifteen hours 177 synagogues were wrecked, 7500 Jewish-owned stores were pillaged and looted. Streets were covered with broken glass. Ninety-one Jewish men were murdered and over 35,000 men, women and children were arrested and sent to concentration camps. The Jewish community was ordered to foot the bill: one million Reichsmark. Taking inflation into account, this is 27 million US dollars today.

1939

One day before the start of her summer holiday, during the last physical education class, Sonja falls and badly hurts her knee. Anton lets her go to Zandvoort as planned; on condition she takes it easy. She promises she will. All she needs is a pile of books and she won't move.

On the beach little Judie builds a mound of sand for Sonja to rest her leg on. At twelve thirty her mother and little Judie walk back to the hotel. They have lunch and bring Sonja back a lunchbox. Halfway through their vacation Anton comes from Amsterdam to check up on her knee.

"Take it easy on the walking and you'll be fine."

In the mean time, Herman like all other refugees is required to report to immigration authorities, to get his monthly residence permit renewed.

In the summer of 1939 Anton and Jet, and their children Judie and Hans, are on vacation in Paris, France. Signs posted everywhere saying, "If you are not French you are an enemy," worry Jet. She suggests, "Anton, let's not go back to Amsterdam. Perhaps we should take a boat to the United States?" but Anton doesn't want to abandon his patients. He wants to take Jet and the children to the harbor of Le Havre, but Jet doesn't want to leave without him.

1939

September 1. Germany attacked Poland. The Dutch government mobilized. There were 3,000 Jewish soldiers in the Dutch army. A large number of German Jews in Holland told horror stories about the fate of Jews in Nazi Germany. Neither the Dutch government, nor the Dutch Jews believed these horror stories. "That's impossible," many reacted, "Germans are a polite and cultured people."

Anton comes home from the hospital with one such horror story from a German Jew he had treated that day.

"He had been arrested and sent to a concentration camp called Dachau." Anton continues, "If his stories are true, we're in for something, but they are probably highly exaggerated." For the most part, the Dutch Jews disregard these doomsday stories. It doesn't concern them. They are convinced those shocking things will never happen in Holland.

Sonja loves singing opera. She knows an array of arias by heart. A friend of her mother's suggests she should get Sonja's voice tested by Cato Engelen Sewing, a well-known opera singer in those days. She goes ahead and has her tested. According to Cato, Sonja has a beautiful voice and she strongly recommends Henrietta to pursue singing lessons for her daughter. Cato's schedule is pretty full at this time but if Sonja is willing to wait, she tells them, they may come back in a few months. "Ninotchka" with Greta Garbo and "First Love" with Deanna Durbin play in the theaters.

1940

Friday May 10. Four o'clock in the morning Nazi Germany invaded Holland. Holland's first reaction was one of disbelief. Holland had not been occupied by a foreign power since Napoleon in 1815. By sunrise, seventy-four divisions of Hitler's army raged through Holland and Belgium. Holland succumbed mostly to Hitler's air force. Twin-engine Junkers JU 88 started bombing Amsterdam airport and other airfields, three-engine JU 52 transport planes carried paratroopers. Above airfields, bridges and other strategic points the airplanes reduced speed to let the paratroopers jump. Crates with weapons and munitions were thrown after them. By early afternoon 1200 air force troops were in charge of most of Holland's airfields. To speed up Holland's surrender, Reich's Field Marshall Herman Göring had the city of Rotterdam bombed. Over eleven hundred inhabitants were killed. On May 14, when the Nazis threatened to bomb the city of Utrecht, the Dutch army, headed by general Winkelman, surrendered. Capitulation papers were signed the following day.

Daybreak. It's five o'clock in the morning. It's been an unusually warm night. The bedroom window is partly open. Monotonous airplane droning wakes them up. Sonja and little Judie go to the window. The sky is swarming with airplanes. She isn't sure what to think of it. Her parents too are awake by now. The four of them watch in disbelief as they see an endless stream of airplanes against the blue sky. The forecast for Friday is sunny and warm. Her father looks worried.

"If only this will end all right. We need to rely on *Kodish Baruchu*." (*Kodish Baruchu*, one of the names for God.) Down in the street they hear the pickle man shouting, "This is it, we are done for!"

Her father nods in agreement.

"The sun won't be shining for us today."

Unable to fall back to sleep, she gets dressed and reads over her homework. Come what may, she's more worried about her exams than the significance of those stupid airplanes. She is intent on passing.

May 12. Prince Bernhard accompanied Princess Juliana, daughters Beatrix and Irene to England and returned to Holland. The following day queen Wilhelmina arrived in England. As a precaution, Princess Juliana and her daughters were sent on to Canada. Two hundred Jews committed suicide.

Sonja passes her high school exams and wants to study nursing. Her mother insists on her getting a secretarial diploma instead. She does so successfully and several months later she gets a job as a secretary. Her boss is more interested in her than in her work. From time to time he buys her a bottle of perfume. Her mother is skeptical but keeps quiet. She's proud of her daughter who hands over two thirds of her earnings every month. Henrietta hasn't wanted to accept any money, but Sonja insists on pulling her own weight.

For the first couple of months into the German invasion nothing changes. Although they know about the humiliating social and economic hardships in Nazi Germany, Dutch Jews are still convinced that these things can't happen in Holland. But then subtly, things start changing. In movie theaters, stores and restaurants, small groups of fanatic national socialists, mostly uneducated and unemployed thugs, start harassing people whom they think look Jewish. If someone looks Jewish, they just walk up to the person and pick a fight. Many Jews are physically attacked and beaten to a pulp. Policemen turn a blind eye. In July, Jews are expelled from the Civil Defense Force. (One of the responsibilities of the CDF is to ensure that curtains are properly closed to prevent enemy aircraft from finding their way. Showing light earns a steep fine). The next directive orders kosher butchers to close down.

June 21, 1940. Hitler and Göring met with French authorities to sign France's surrender. The signing took place in the woods of Compiègne, the same location and in the same train car where Germany had surrendered in 1918, at the end of World War I.

In 1941 around the Easter holiday, the town of Zandvoort was the first town in Holland to apply the anti-Jewish directive that made renting rooms to Jews against the law. Members of the national socialist party harassed Jewish kids in the center of town and on the beach.

Zandvoort went into history as the first town to post signs, "NO JEWS ALLOWED."

Since they don't go on vacation any more, Henrietta surprises her daughters with brand new dazzling-looking bicycles. They love their spotless shiny bicycles and their disappointment is quickly overcome. Sundays after cleaning up her room, Sonja and her friends ride their bikes to the park where they enjoy a picnic and a swim in the lake. Henrietta doesn't realize that Herman is also part of the group. At six o'clock in the evening he takes Sonja back. They say their goodbyes behind the familiar wall.

In the fall all Jewish magazines and newspapers are shut down, except for the Jewish Weekly, which in time the Nazis will underhandedly use as their official mouthpiece. In November all Jewish public servants, schoolteachers and university professors are fired. In December it becomes against the law for Jews to employ non-Jews. Not everybody obeys the new rules. Mrs. Roderigues, Henrietta's domestic help, is lucky enough to be only half Jewish. All these rules and regulations do not affect her. She courageously disagrees with all this German nonsense and refuses to resign. She has worked for Henrietta since the time Sonja and little Judie wore diapers. She loves them as if they are her own girls.

Sonja is close to both her parents, yet her father is her absolute hero. She is proud to help him anyway she can. Her secretarial diploma proves to have been a smart move. She's a good typist and she takes good shorthand. For her eighteenth birthday she gets a portable Continental typewriter. Jacob's business has grown and she loves to help him with his business correspondence. She also helps him by carrying orders of fabric bolts to the shipping company van Gent & Loos.

1941

 January 8 changes a Wednesday afternoon tradition. Henrietta and her daughters go to the movie theater to watch, "The Immortal Waltz," with Milizia Korjus. Without knowing it, this is the last time they see a movie together. Four days later the Dutch Association of Theater Owners puts a sign outside the entrance of every theater, NO JEWS ALLOWED. By now, anti-Jewish directives follow each other quickly. Jews need to hand in their radios. From now on, Jewish attorneys, doctors and pharmacists are only allowed to service Jewish patients and clients. Signs with NO JEWS ALLOWED appear in windows of hotels, cafés, restaurants, swimming pools, other sport facilities, museums, libraries, parks and markets. Lots of other public places become off limits. For Jews living in Amsterdam it is illegal to leave the city. A few months later Jews all over Holland are ordered to move to Amsterdam. Most Jews still think that if it doesn't get any worse, they'll be able to live with these rules.

 All Dutch people of fourteen years and older had to register. They were issued an I.D. card to be carried on them at all times. Jews got an additional 'J' stamped on theirs. Suddenly it was easy to tell the Jews from the non-Jews.

 At the German club some of Herman's friends disappear to go into hiding, others go into the resistance. Herman is not interested in politics and refuses several times to be recruited.

 The Nazis founded the Jewish Council in Holland, after Jewish Councils in Poland, Germany, Austria and Czechoslovakia proved an efficient strategy. Council members were all Jews. On behalf of the Nazis the Council carried out directives against other Jews. Let it be clear that the Nazis ran and wholly controlled the Council. Its members were no more than puppets or errand boys doing the Nazis' dirty work. The Council as a whole cooperated with the Nazis.

They hoped it would save lives. Besides, refusing an order meant deportation. The Council's first task was to keep the Jews advised of the ever-increasing deluge of new directives. They were responsible that the new rules published in the Jewish Weekly, were obeyed. It was against the law for non-Jews to read the Jewish Weekly. Consequently, the general population had little or no knowledge of the predicament the Jews found themselves in. Sadly, solidarity was therefore out of the question.

In November, all foreign Jews were ordered to report for work in Germany. The Council had to pick and choose what families were deported and in what order. It was an emotional affair, although strong ties with the refugees had not taken root. Once all the foreign Jews had been deported the Dutch Jews were next. Family and friendships made the Council members' choices extremely difficult, if not impossible.

The Jewish Council comprised several departments; the Expositur, *or* Expo *operated as an intermediary between the Jewish Council and the Center for Jewish Emigration (Zentralstelle). For the main part German Jews worked at the Expo, which supervised deportations. The Center for Jewish Emigration was responsible for securing the number of Jews for deportation. Doing the Nazis' dirty work, the Council was responsible which Jews were to be sacrificed first. For example, if the Center for Jewish Emigration wanted to deport a thousand Jews on a specific date, the Council had to deliver a thousand Jews. The Nazi strategy worked. Jews were selecting Jews for deportation. The Center for Jewish Emigration organized the deportations out of Holland, while the Expo concerned itself with logistics.*

After numerous intrigues, SS Hauptsturmfürer *(captain) Ferdinant Aus der Fünten took charge of the Center for Jewish Emigration. Aus der Fünten was from Vienna, as was Herman's boss Sluzker. They knew each other from high school. Both had been smart, disciplined and focused students. Although they had not been friends, they had respected each other. At High school they had been on opposing debate teams and their skillful debates usually attracted ample spectators.*

SS Captain Aus der Funten put Sluzker in charge of the Expo. *Sluzker became the bridge between Aus der Fünten, head of the Center for Jewish Emigration and the Jewish Council, an extremely powerful position. Sluzker took Herman, by now his right hand man and protégé, with him.*

For a young man oblivious to politics Herman finds himself in a much-envied position. Being in charge of the Expo, Sluzker puts together and supervises the deportations lists. This basically entails preparing deportation lists, handling exemption requests, supplying the number of Jews that Aus der Fünten demands, and much more. At first Aus der Fünten pretends to be agreeable and lets Sluzker gleefully bargain down the number of deportees.

In March 1941, Jewish businesses were expropriated from their owners and put under German or German sympathizers' supervision.

The National Bureau of Textile Distribution cancels Jacob's permit and orders his supplies to be confiscated. Ownership is being transferred to S.I. de Vries. Jacob is left without an income.

The seventeen and a half thousand employees of the Jewish Council who were working on deporting other Jews, their next of kin and their personal friends, were exempt from deportation. Jews married to non-Jewish spouses, Jews converted to Christianity, Jews with 'Aryan blood,' Portuguese Jews, Jews in Germany working in the war industry, and Jews working in the diamond industry were granted a Sperr stamp, an exemption stamp, on their ID. The Nazis knew from experience that Jews with Sperr stamps would feel safe and not go into hiding. In reality, however, an exemption stamp only meant temporary reprieve from deportation. "Those lucky enough to have a stamp were deported after a few months, after all." (Hans Knoop, *The Jewish Council)*

There are two kinds of lists. The first contains names and addresses of Jews marked for transport. The second contains names of those who are *"Sperred."* Aus der Fünten wants updated lists on his desk at all times. After Aus der Fünten discusses the names on the lists with Sluzker, Sluzker hands them to Herman to update them. Herman carries these confidential papers from Sluzker to Aus der Fünten and back to the *Expo* on a daily basis. He updates the lists and is able to add or take off a name here and there. Aus der Fünten seems to like this blond, good-looking young man. Every so often he remarks, "Your German is excellent. You don't sound Jewish, you don't look Jewish. Are you sure you are Jewish?" Herman knows what Aus der Fünten is getting at. Herman believes that Chaim Rosenstein is not his biological father. Whether he actually knows that his father is an Aryan soldier and that he is the product of a one-night stand, remains a question. He does suspect something, because his mother never did give him a straight answer. Nevertheless, it does not seem a good idea for him to be sharing his suspicions with Aus der Fünten. He has kept quiet about it so far. Not being Jewish would have been a reason for the Dutch government to deny him refugee status and cancel his residence permit. Every time he has wanted to tell Sonja, he changes his mind. How would she deal with it? Worse, how would her parents react were they to find out that his father is an Aryan? One day he will tell her, when the war is over. At this time, during the occupation, he doesn't want to be mistaken for an Aryan, but looking and sounding like an Aryan works to his advantage, for now. At the Center for Jewish Emigration they think he works for Aus der Fünten.

In the course of 1941 and 1942 Jews were ordered to close their bank accounts and register their money, stocks and all other valuables with a fictitious branch of an existing Jewish bank, the Lippmann-Rosenthal Bank (LiRo). The Nazis kept the name Lippmann-Rosenthal on purpose, as not to cause any suspicion abroad. Consequently, foreign banks continued doing business with the Lippmann-Rosenthal bank. The original bank remained at the same address but was kept totally separate from the new fictitious branch. Because deposits, debits and monthly statements looked official, the Dutch Jews did not panic. On top of that, the Jewish Council kept saying that it was imperative to follow the new rules. After the Jews deposited their money, stocks and valuables into new accounts, their accounts were frozen. The Jews were being choked financially. The Jewish Council received small amounts of money to be distributed amongst the members of the Jewish community. It was the familiar carrot and stick tactic. Just as everything felt hopeless, there seemed to be a way out, somewhat.

When Herman goes down to the station to renew his December residence permit, a Dutch policeman tells him in a friendly manner that he doesn't need a permit anymore. Better yet, "you won't be needing your passport anymore either. I'll keep that for you. Thank you very much."

"They won't be sending me back to Germany. I'm allowed to stay," he tells Sonja self-assuredly. "There's no need to worry anymore."

He works hard and issues increasingly more *Sperr* stamps. Sonja doesn't know exactly what he does, for he talks little about his work.

November 1941. Hitler's Munich speech: "Germany will never capitulate." The following month he appointed himself commander-in-chief of the army.

In December of 1941 Jacob receives a letter in the mail stating the conditions that "allow" him to open a bank account with the Lippmann-Rosenthal Bank. Paragraph 2 states: "We look after your money as if it's our own." Paragraph 14 states: "The above conditions are binding according to the regulations of the Federal Commissioner of the occupied Dutch territories." Jacob has no choice but to report his assets.

At the end of 1941, Willy Lages, former Mayer of the city of Lübeck and currently heading the Sicherheits Polizei, the SiPo, (Security Police) was put in charge of the Center for Jewish Emigration. Aus der Fünten continued to run the Center, but from then on he had to answer to Lages. Aus der Fünten and Lages had a history of infighting and backbiting. They had been discrediting each other in Berlin for years. They fought each other for Hitler's attention and competed over control of Holland, triggering catastrophic consequences. Lages found Aus der Funten too lenient towards the "Jewish problem." The conflict between them escalated. Lages didn't hide his hatred and openly harbored contempt for anyone from the Aus der Fünten camp.

Sonja checks into the hospital to have an appendectomy. Out of the hospital and having recovered, she and Herman make a train trip to Den Bosch to visit her uncle Maurits. They have special travel papers. There are very few Jews to be seen around and Herman decides that it's better not to travel anymore, unless they absolutely have to.

1942

January 20. On a freezing winter day during an official lunch in the Berlin suburb of Wannsee, about fifteen high-ranking Nazi officers were trying to find a solution to the "Jewish problem."

Europe was ridding itself of the Jews, but logistically they couldn't be killed fast enough. A bullet or two per person proved too costly and too time consuming. The concentration camps were packed. Consequently there was a storage problem. By the time the men were ready for dessert, their storage problem was solved. Working towards greater efficiency, they decided to replace manual executions by means of bullets, with gas chambers. To shorten the walking distance to the gas chambers they planned to extend railroad tracks right into the camps. It would make the procedure more efficient. Today's lunch in this luxurious Wannsee mansion was to affect the life of every Jew in occupied Europe, including that of Sonja and Herman and her family.

Ghettos were sealed off, densely populated, run-down areas of a city, which Jews were not allowed to leave. They were full of lice, rats and contagious diseases. There was a lack of food and many adults and children starved to death. Dead bodies lying about in the streets were hurled onto wheelbarrows and thrown into mass graves.

When Herman returns home from a long day at work, Aunt Bettie sits waiting for him in a dark living room. He can tell something is wrong. He turns the light on. She motions silently to a postcard on the table.

He sees a red cross on the front of the card.

"Why would the Red Cross send me a card?" Unenthusiastically he picks the card up. He recognizes his mother's handwriting. He reads that his mother, sister, stepfather and newborn stepbrother have moved to the ghetto of Lodz. Herman, however, has no concept of these circumstances. He gazes at the red cross.

"Perhaps someone working for the Red Cross gave her the card." He doesn't understand why they moved.

"Perhaps," he says to his aunt, "they wanted to move to a bigger place."

1942. In Amsterdam a group of Jews was picked up from the streets and put into labor camps in Holland.

Herman is constantly retyping both lists. He deletes names from the transport list and adds them to the *Sperr* list. He has to work fast and carefully. If Aus der Fünten is in his office, Herman strikes up a conversation with an assistant or secretary until Aus der Fünten leaves. When the coast is clear, Herman says, "I'll go ahead and put this paperwork on his desk." He then replaces the approved lists with the ones he has revised. This way a young man with no interest in politics tries to save many Jewish lives. Sadly, in most cases the delay was only temporary.

There was a disturbance in the street; a couple of Jews were being assaulted and they fought back. Policemen who were standing right there, enjoying a smoke, turned their backs. People passing by were ordered to move on. Punished for fighting back, the Jewish neighborhood was blocked off and about four hundred Jews were rounded up and deported to a concentration camp called Mauthausen.

Sonja and Herman meet regularly at Gerdi's. Then something happens they have been afraid of all along. In March of 1942 Sonja thinks she might be pregnant. Getting married is out of the question. Her mother will never allow it. Herman thinks sadly that these are no times to have a baby. He has a *Sperr* and hopes to get Sonja one too, but what if they are called up to work in what the Germans euphemistically call "the East?" A baby? No, they can't run that risk. They find a doctor willing to give her some pills. She needs to talk about it, but she doesn't dare to approach her mother. Their downstairs neighbor, Jettie, has a three-year-old. She'll probably understand. She goes downstairs to ask Jettie for advice. They have tea and talk about her work. She looks at Jettie's wedding picture hanging on the wall in the living room and changes her mind about asking advice.

"That's how I want to dress when Herman and I get married, with a beautiful long white veil."

"How is Herman?"

"He's fine. We're going to the theater this afternoon to see the *Bajadère.*"

She finishes her tea and goes back upstairs. She finds her mother in her bedroom, the contents of her purse scattered on her bed.

"What are those pills?" Her mother yells at the top of her lungs. Sonja starts to cry.

"I am late."

She is punished and not allowed to leave her room. Her mother calls Jacob. She asks him to come home immediately. When Herman rings the bell at two o'clock, Jacob answers the door. From her bedroom Sonja hears bits and pieces of their conversation.

"Hello, sir. I am here to pick up Sonja. We are going to the theater," she hears him say politely.

"There is no going to the theater and you are never to see my daughter again... immigration police... across the border to Germany..." She has never ever heard her father talk that way. She hears the front door open and close. She cries for hours, eventually crying herself to sleep. That evening she gets her period.

It has taken Jacob five years to build a thriving business and a comfortable life. His family doesn't want for anything. The girls are healthy. Sonja graduated with high marks and little Judie is doing well in school. To his wife Jacob mentions several times, "If we continue like this we will be able to move to the south of Amsterdam." For Henrietta, who has quietly been waiting for that day, it is great news. A bigger home is the only request on her wish list.

But now Jacob's business has been confiscated and turned over to a Nazi collaborator. His life has come to a sudden halt. He has no income and he can't access his money. He sells the last bit of fabric he has in stock. Is he still thinking, like most Jews in Holland, that everything is going to be fine?

Every week the Jewish Weekly publicizes new anti-Jewish laws. When Jews may no longer drive, Anton takes his car to a friend who owns a garage. After the war, when Anton went to pick his car up, the friend demanded thousands of guilders as a parking fee.

When Jews are ordered to turn in their bicycles, Sonja and Judie sadly surrender their bikes. Jews have to be inside between eight o'clock at night and six o'clock in the morning. Since using public transport for Jews is against the law, Sonja walks thirty minutes to Gerdi's where she meets Herman for half an hour before rushing back home again. Herman has a *Sperr* and is allowed to be outside until nine o'clock.

Jews all over Holland were now required to move to Amsterdam. Their isolation had almost been accomplished. They were being swept together as it were with a broom and dustpan and now it was only a matter of time until they were discarded as dirt into the trash can, or in their case the gas chambers and ovens. Leaving Amsterdam without official papers was against the law. Through the Jewish Weekly, the Nazis announced that the Jews were being sent to Germany and Poland to work. Once again the Jewish Council advised the Jewish community to follow orders. By cooperating they were hoping to be spared worse. The Jewish Council, its employees and family members did not qualify for deportation, as yet.

The buzzword is: *Sperr* stamp. News spreads like wildfire that Herman is the man. He becomes extremely busy. Once in a while Sonja asks him what he thinks about the situation. He assures her that everything is fine. One day, when Herman walks Sonja to work, they meet an excited Anneliese Lustig. She's been lucky for a change.

"Lucky? How?" Sonja asks.

"I received my orders to report today. I've always wanted to travel, so I volunteered at the Center for Jewish Emigration; I want to see the world. They are sending me to Poland." Years later, Sonja realizes that Annliese Lustig was one of the very first to go to Poland, straight to the gas chamber.

The order to report listed what you were allowed to take on your trip: 1 suitcase or backpack, 1 pair of rubber boots, 2 pairs of socks, 2 pieces of underwear, 2 shirts, 1 pair of work pants, 2 woolen blankets, 2 sets of sheets, 1 bowl, 1 mug, 1 spoon and 1 sweater, towel and toiletries. Lots of people had their backpack ready next to their bed.

Sonja suffers her yearly recurring bladder infection and has to stay in bed. Little Judie secretly shuttles notes to and from Herman. When she comes back from one of her missions, she describes in detail how much Herman talks about missing her. After Sonja is well again, Herman tells Gerdi to call Sonja to arrange for them to meet. Gerdi makes the call but Henrietta answers the phone and pretends to be Sonja.

"Yes Gerdi, how are you?" Gerdi knows she is talking to Henrietta and plays along.

"Sonja, are you coming this afternoon?"

Henrietta asks, "Is Herman coming too?"

"Herman?" Gerdi answers, "I haven't seen him in ages."

1942

In April the Nazi government decided that by December of 1942, 15,000 Dutch Jews had to have been deported. In May the Jewish Weekly announced that all Jews were to sew a yellow Star of David on the left chest of each piece of clothing. Disobedience meant deportation. Costs of the stars were deducted from their clothing rations. Wanting to show solidarity, some non-Jews wore a star too. They were apprehended and sent to a concentration camp.

Henrietta doesn't waver for a second. "If we are caught without a star, we will be worse off." Together with Sonja she goes to the Jewish agency and buys the required number of stars. Instructions specify the exact position on the garments.

Sunday June 14, 1942 the Council mails out the first batch of envelopes containing orders to report. Last names A through D, under the age of forty are to present themselves at a given location. Two days later, at 10:30 in the morning Sonja is at work, when the phone rings. Her mother cries, "Two orders to report arrived in the mail today, one for you and one for little Judie. You are leaving July 15 on the first transport to Camp Westerbork. Uncle Philip," she cries, "came by to tell us that Sara and Beppie received theirs too."

Sonja reacts immediately, "I am going to get a hold of Herman. He'll be able to help."

"Herman? Are you still in touch with him?"

"Mother, now is not the time."

"Can Herman stop this?"

"Perhaps he can. I need to get those orders to Herman as soon as possible. Can father get them to me?"

"He's already on his way." She hangs up and immediately the phone rings again. It is Herman.

"Hi Sonja, I can't have lunch with you today, they are conducting a *razzia* (a sweep or round up for the purpose of mass arrests) in the center of Amsterdam. Whatever you do, stay away from the center."

She tells him that she and little Judie have received their orders to report.

"Get them to me as soon as you can, but be careful." Before he hangs up he adds quickly, "Call your father. Tell him to stay indoors."

She hangs up. The door opens and her father enters. He quickly closes the door behind him. She notices that he looks upset and that he doesn't want to show it. He hands her the two envelopes. She tells him that she just talked to Herman and that he might be able to help. Jacob hesitates.

"Can we accept his help after what happened? I will discuss it with Rabbi de Hond."

She warns that Herman just told her he should go home and stay home. "Father, please be careful."

He kisses her and leaves. She puts on her coat and hurriedly counts to a hundred before she leaves. Alert, she carries her purse over her left chest, hiding the yellow Star of David. A surge of adrenaline rushes through her. If she is caught, it'll be the end of her. She needs to get to Herman. His office is across town. She doesn't dare to take the Vijzelstraat. She hurries from the Kloveniersburgwal to the Doelenstraat. She sees a horse pulling a cart. It belongs to van Gent & Loos, the shipping company her father used for shipping his fabrics. Nervously she asks the man on the box if he'll let her ride along under the canvas.

"If you can manage to climb in," he answers while spitting out a shot of tobacco. It's not easy to climb in, but she's agile enough. Anxiously she sits among the parcels. It seems to take forever. From time to time she peeks out through an opening in the canvass. She recognizes the Beethovenstraat. The man on the box yells something unintelligible. The cart stops. Not wasting a second she jumps out and runs. He cracks his whip and the horse starts walking. She keeps running until she reaches the office of the Expo. Inside it's a hectic scene. The hallway is crowded and noisy. Herman isn't there. Nobody knows where he is. She decides to wait. By four o'clock, she cringes. She's been waiting since noon. She has to return to the office. She is about to give the two envelopes to a young man who promises to give them to Herman, when she sees Herman making his way towards her through the crowded hallway.

"Give me those." He takes the envelopes from her. He is hurried. People are calling him. "Everything's fine, Son. Tell your mother not to worry. I'm so sorry, but I couldn't help your cousins Sara and Beppie. They have to report. Tell your uncle it's better that they go just the two of them; he should not see them off at the Central Station."

That evening she tells her parents the good news. Well, it's not all that good really. Sara and Beppie are going to be deported. Henrietta breaks out in tears. Her daughters have narrowly escaped, but Sara and Beppie and all children and adolescents between 5 and twenty-five years old are leaving from Amsterdam Central Station at half past midnight. Hours after their bedtime they will arrive at Camp Westerbork, unaware of how much worse things are going to get.

The following day Jacob invites Rabbi de Hond for a cup of tea. The rabbi suggests Jacob should let Sonja and Herman marry.

"Lots of young couples are getting married. With the same last name they will be deported together. Plus, if Herman is your son-in-law you may unquestionably accept his help."

"How are we going to verify who this young man really is?" Jacob wants to know.

"Times are different now. I hear good things about him. Give him a chance." Sonja, not the shy type, is speechless. How can she ever thank Rabbi de Hond?

Marrying a refugee gets everybody talking and every one has an opinion. Nevertheless, they marry on Wednesday August 12, 1942 during a civil ceremony in an administrative office of the Jewish Agency. A Jewish Agency civil servant marries some forty Jewish couples at the same time. Sonja and Herman would love to spend a few days in Den Bosch but leaving Amsterdam is against the law. Even Herman's papers won't safeguard him. These aren't the best of times to celebrate. Yet, Sonja is happy. She is finally Herman's wife. Celebrations can wait. Herman goes back to work and Sonja returns to her office.

Aus der Fünten and Lages had a quota to fill, or there would be trouble with Eichmanns's office in Berlin. The process of sending out notices through the regular mail proved too slow. Worried that the Center for Jewish Emigration couldn't meet their December target of fifteen thousand Jews, notices were now delivered by hand. Two Dutch policemen delivered them after eight o'clock in the evening. At first they rang the bell politely, handed over the notice and bade the recipient a good evening. The recipients had a few days to pack. Soon enough, however, the bell ringing turned into malicious banging on the front door. If the door wasn't opened fast enough, the police kicked it in and ordered the residents to come along immediately. If elderly or sick people were already in bed sleeping, the police woke them up by emptying a bucket of cold water over them. They then dragged them into the street in their pajamas. Neighbors saw little; their curtains were closed. The terror intensified. The Dutch were coerced into distancing themselves from their Jewish neighbors.

The OrPo (Ordnungspolizei, Order Police) helped Dutch police in forcing Jews from their homes.

"Tonight chasing Jews, it was a very successful night. I think that these last few weeks I must have caught a few hundred Jews. Returned home this morning at three thirty," an enthusiastic Jew hunter declared. (Hans Knoop, The Jewish Council) There were policemen who let their "target" get away or they warned them in advance. However, most of the police "did their duty." Between Amsterdam and Hooghalen, the little train station near concentration Camp Westerbork, trains kept running on time. At the camp, the OrPo handed their 'cargo' over to camp personnel who were Jewish prisoners.

"We are escorted like cattle to be killed and to vanish," Rabbi Abraham Toncman noted down in the minutes of the synagogue in Pekela, a northern town in Groningen. (Hans Knoop, *The Jewish Council*)

Nobody knows exactly what working in "the East" actually means, but their gut feeling tells them it isn't good. Thousands of Jews try to get a *Sperr* stamp. Herman is busier than ever. He manages to remove names from deportation lists and add them to the Sperr lists.

Jacob and Henrietta never do receive their notice to report dated August 3, 1942. Instead Jacob receives a letter from the Jewish Council, Expo department:

"Herewith we let you know that on grounds of your working for the Jewish Council in Amsterdam you will not be required to register for work in Germany. We have kept your notice number 13108/o7."

It's highly probable that Herman wrote and signed Sluzker's name on this Sperr letter. Jacob's brother Philip and his wife Clara do receive their notices. On August 3, 1942 they report to the authorities. The same day they are sent to concentration camp Westerbork.

To capture more Jewish families, the Nazis organized more and bigger razzias. They closed off whole neighborhoods by opening bridges. This way all Jews were systematically tracked down, picked up and deported. Razzias were accompanied by verbal abuse and physical violence.

Jacob is desperate. The situation seems hopeless. Against all odds, he and others in his situation are still hoping that these setbacks are of a temporary nature. Financially he sees no way out. On August 4, 1942 he writes the Lippmann-Rosenthal bank "Politely but urgently I request your help, as my financial means are totally exhausted and I don't know how to carry on. Please accommodate me as soon as possible."

A few days later he receives a conformation letter from the bank. To pacify him, they send him a check for 600 guilders, but he is ordered to record all his valuables; silver dishes, silver egg holders, silver chains, rings, etc.

The next check he receives is for half the amount. They are caught like rats in a trap. There seems to be no way out. No Jew feels safe anymore. Those in hiding are afraid of being informed on and many of them decide to report themselves. They are punished as soon as they do and deported, as are their hosts.

Going into hiding was a drama in itself. There were all sorts of problems. Most commonly the Jews in hiding were betrayed by treacherous family members or nosy neighbors. Hosts often blackmailed their guests by wanting more money than the initially agreed upon amount, but Jews had no access to their money and sometimes they were asked to leave. Although parents refused to relinquish their children, they often got separated. Jewish or host children often couldn't keep their mouths shut, this jeopardized the host families, leading to the most horrendous consequences. Hiding together with others and not getting along created its own set of problems. Without going into detail, it is not an exaggeration to call the hosts who were hiding Jews "heroes." Many hosts paid for their heroic deeds with their lives.

Judie, daughter of Anton and Jet, is about to go into hiding. Before disappearing, she visits Jacob and Henrietta suggesting she take little Judie with her.

"No way, absolutely not. Far too dangerous."

Henrietta doesn't want to hear about it.

"You're jeopardizing all of us. Perhaps it's better that you don't come here anymore."

Jacob doesn't usually oppose his wife, but this time he throws her a look before turning to Judie.

"Judie, you will always be welcome in this house."

Judie leaves in a hurry. She never sees her aunt and uncle again. Not much later Judie's brother Hans goes into hiding. Finally Anton, who has not wanted to abandon his patients, buckles under Jet's pressure. He and Jet disappear too.

The Dutch Theater, (De Hollandsche Schouwburg), built in 1892, was located in the nightlife area of the old Jewish neighborhood in Amsterdam. The first two years the Theater was used to perform operas. After that it was mostly used for stage plays. In 1941 the Nazis changed its name to the Jewish Theater. After the name change, Jewish musicians and Jewish artists played for Jewish audiences only. In 1942 and 1943 the Nazis used the Theater as a storage facility for the departing Jews, a central point of assembly for all those who had received their notices and were about to be deported. The Nazis paid for the rental of the Theater with money stolen from Jewish bank accounts. The Theater had become a sinister site of peril, disaster and intense grief and sorrow.

"The Theater had been wrecked. The stage had been stripped from backdrops and scenery. It looked as if the place had been burglarized. Ropes hanging from the lighting bridge looked like hangman's nooses. Paintings and statues had disappeared. Auditorium and orchestra chairs had been ripped out and placed alongside the walls. All lights, except for the emergency lights, were removed. The auditorium

was packed with crying babies, whining children wanting to go home and desperate adults waiting their turn to be deported. Time and again new groups entered the auditorium, surprised, exhausted, packed and ready to leave." (H. Wielek, *De Oorlog die Hitler won*)

Some spent several hours there, others days or weeks. There was no clean water or food. Toilets were filthy. Personal belongings were scattered chaotically through the auditorium. The last train for Camp Westerbork left Amsterdam at the end of September 1943. On board were the members of the Jewish Council. They had been unable to save themselves. The doors of the Theater closed in November. The clamor and commotion of the previous months would echo through the building for years. For the Nazis the Jewish problem was solved. Thousands of men, women and children had been deported from the Theater to concentration camp Westerbork, and from there on to their death. Few survived 'the East.' Of the 110.000 Dutch Jews, the Nazis killed 105.000.

Once inside the auditorium there was no escape possible. If your name still appeared on the deportation list, it was your turn and your number was up. Guards escorted the miserable group dragging their belongings onto a streetcar and accompanied them to Amsterdam Central Station or Amsterdam Muiderpoort station. In the very beginning, before the details were worked out, Jews and non-Jews sat next to each other. The non-Jewish men were mostly on their way to work, the women were girlfriends on their way to enjoy a cup of coffee together. They got on with their lives as usual.

"When yet another group of weary Jews with suitcases, guarded by a couple of uniforms, got in, passengers would sigh, because they were in a hurry. Sometimes, when the guards weren't watching, a Jew would hand a passenger a note. Sometimes the passenger took it, nodded and quickly looked away. They were not allowed to talk to each other." (Guus Meershoek, *Dienaren van het Gezag*)

Soldiers of the SS, (SS members were originally black shirted personal bodyguards of Hitler. Later they became part of a political police. The name Schutzstaffel (defense echelon) was abbreviated to SS written as lighting flashes in runic characters) assisted by members of the national socialist movement, (the NSB), guarded the theater. Dutch collaborators that helped hunt down Jews in hiding dropped the captured Jews off at the theater. Prisoners were prohibited from talking to the guards. Questions were only to be addressed to Jewish Council members.

1942

October 11, a little before one o'clock, Sonja, her parents and little Judie walk to the synagogue on the Jonas Daniel Meijerplein. It's the day of her *choppa*, her Jewish wedding, with Herman. She is excited but it's not a particularly happy day. The Jewish Weekly is filled with advertisements for backpacks. Relatives, friends and acquaintances have gone into hiding. So too have her dearest Uncle Anton, his wife Jet and their children Judie and Hans.

Despite the hard times, the *shul* is packed. Herman's aunt Bettie and her daughter Jennie are present, Rabbi de Hond with his wife and kids and Mr. and Mrs. Gans attend. Mrs. Gans is happy for Sonja, but privately she reflects that her son Hansfried would probably make Sonja a better husband. Jacob and Henrietta most likely agreed. A frugal party with coffee and cake follows in hotel Hiegentlich in Amsterdam. Mrs. Gans insists on Sonja and Herman moving in with her and her husband. After all, their sons are not living at home anymore.

Their new address becomes Apollolaan 97 corner Beethovenstraat. Mrs. Gans feels a sense of security that Herman, who works for the Expo, lives with her and her husband. A copy of Sonja's wedding photo is strategically placed on the cupboard in the living room. Sonja often looks at it, remembering Jettie's wedding photo. Her dream has come true. She has finally married her high school sweetheart. Herman wants to pay rent, but Mrs. Gans not only refuses, she insists they eat and share all their meals together.

Mrs. and Mr. Gans are absolutely wonderful. Except for the constant threat of being uprooted, these are relatively happy months. Without realizing it, by marrying Herman, Sonja moved from C to R on the deportation list, delaying her fate. She often drops in on her parents, even though being outside is becoming increasingly dangerous. Shortly after they are married she becomes pregnant. Her mother thinks it's a bad idea to have a child under these circumstances. Herman agrees. An acquaintance refers her to a doctor who suggests Sonja sees his son, who is also a doctor. The son terminates the pregnancy and by doing so he saves her life, because pregnant women when deported and upon arrival in an extermination camp, are immediately sent to the gas chambers. Years later, during happier times, that same doctor will help Sonja with the birth of her four children.

Mrs. Gans hears of a hiding place for little Judie. She discusses it with Jacob and Henrietta. After careful deliberation they now agree. Henrietta misses little Judie terribly but is distracted by other agonizing matters. She collects the most valuable of their belongings and gives them to Mrs. Rodrigues to hold on to. With the neighbors watching her coming and going, it has become far too dangerous for this extraordinarily brave cleaning lady to keep on working for Henrietta. They hug and cry when they finally say good-bye.

Little Judie is having a hard time at her hiding place. She is forced to eat pork and cries a lot. Henrietta decides to bring her little one home.

November 1942, on Sonja's twentieth birthday, Mrs. Gans and Sonja are in the living room when they look out of the window and see an agitated Jacob rushing towards them. He is by himself. It's too far for Henrietta to walk. Jacob explains that Sam Olij, a well-known boxer and now a policeman who tracks down Jews, has paid them a visit. He wanted to take them in but he saw Herman and

Sonja's wedding photo and asked, "Who is that? I know that guy." Her mother answered, "That's my son-in-law and my daughter."

"Is that right," Sam Olij had said, "That's your son-in-law. Well, good day then. Come on," he had said to his partner, "We're at the wrong address."

"They left, but your mother is terribly worried." Appalled and anxious over what had happened, Henrietta decides to have her polio foot operated upon. Just in case she has to walk, she'll handle the traveling better. Released from the hospital after fourteen days, she walks a little better, making her feel a bit more confident and optimistic about the future.

1943

Phone calls, traveling, associating with, visiting and marrying non-Jews were all against the law now. Shopping was allowed between 2 and 4 in a few assigned stores. Those lucky enough to have found a hiding-place have disappeared by now; many who hadn't, saw no way out and committed suicide.

Herman still doesn't know exactly what happens to the people who are "labor deployed" to the East, but he has questions. The Nazis insist these people are going to work, but what about the babies, the sick and the elderly? Surely they can't work. Working twenty hours a day for Sluzker and semi-assisting Aus der Fünten, Herman has little or no time to sit down to think about it.

Council staff members wear armbands for identification purposes. Herman doesn't. He knows the guards and, more importantly, they know him. They think he works for Aus der Fünten. With his Aryan looks he can just about enter and exit anywhere without being questioned. Policemen and guards greet him thinking he's one of them. He goes about his business, dividing his time between the Center for Jewish Emigration, where he removes names from deportation lists and the Jewish Theater, where he successfully negotiates updated deportation lists. He helps people escape by walking them past the SS guards out of the Theater.

Families are stuck inside the Theater from a couple of days to several weeks. They make do without personal hygiene. The toilets are filthy, there's no toilet paper and food and water are in short supply. Those who find the dirty conditions and the constant whining of the children too much to handle, are impatient and can't wait to be sent on. Herman helps the wretched and distressed. He promises to deliver their last-minute scribbled notes to family or friends. Sonja hardly sees him. When he comes home it's late and he is dead tired. He doesn't talk about his work.

Hitler: "The Jewish problem can only be solved by brute force."

Jacob receives a letter from the Jewish Council. They have decided to give him a 'benefit' of 250 guilders a month.

"Payments will be made in two installments. Although we hope that the total of both installments will equal the above-mentioned maximum, we need to advise you emphatically that it will depend on circumstances beyond our control whether this indeed will be the case."

June 11 Jacob receives 125 guilders. Nine days later he, his wife and little Judie are taken from their home and sent in a cattle car to Camp Westerbork.

Dr. C. Blüth is a respected Jewish Council staff member. Blüth has a privileged position. He is a problem solver who travels between Camp Westerbork and Amsterdam. Herman knows him from his days at the Committee for Jewish Refugees. Blüth lives around the corner from Mr. and Mrs. Gans.

When Sonja hands in her bike, she must give up her job. The walk to work is too far. She asks Herman if he knows of any other jobs. Herman checks with Blüth. Blüth's maid has had to resign because she is not Jewish. So Sonja starts doing some simple house cleaning for Mrs. Blüth. She dusts a bit and does the dishes. Her getting the job is more as a favor to Herman. It is a good thing

Blüth lives nearby, because by now walking in the street is extremely dangerous. When it comes up, she tells Blüth she has her typing diploma and she owns a typewriter. On condition she brings her own typewriter, Blüth manages to get her a job at the *Expo*. It's a short walk, just around the corner. At the *Expo* she starts working for Mr. Heilblut. The letters she types for Heilblut vary in contents from hopeful to carefully giving advice.

"Go ahead and join your husband. He is waiting for you," Sonja hears Heilblut tell Mrs. Aldewereld, a friend of her mother's.

"Surely not," Mrs. Aldewereld tells her daughters Carrie and Beppie. They go into hiding and survive the war. Mr. Aldewereld doesn't.

Herman puts her at ease, insisting everything is going to be fine.

"We work at the *Expo*. They need us, don't worry about a thing." Those were his exact words.

1943

March. Not enough Jews were reporting for "work in the East." Many had gone into hiding. Consequently, deportations were stagnating. Head money or awards were now being paid for the capture of every Jew. The award was seven and a half guilders a head. That is about forty US dollars today. Head money was paid to a core group of about fifty men, volunteers, who traveled relentlessly throughout Holland to ultimately trace about eight to nine thousand Jewish men, women, children and babies. (Ad van Liempt, 'Kopgeld')

Klaartje Richter's parents are longtime patients of Anton's; over the years they have become friends. Klaartje is married to David Horneman. Klaartje and David receive their notices to report. Klaartje tells Sonja that their time has come. Sonja thinks she can help and asks Sluzker for two *Sperr* stamps. A few days later when Sonja goes to drop the *Sperrs* off, Klaartje and David are gone. She must have missed them by a couple of hours. Sonja never heard from them again, as if they never existed. A few days later Freddie Michel, a friend of little Judie's drops by.

"Can you help me? I want to go to France." Before Herman can answer, Sonja gives him the two *Sperrs*, meant for Klaartje and David. Freddie and his wife survived the war.

THE END OF THE BEGINNING.

April. It's a hot summer night. Mr. and Mrs. Gans and Sonja are eating dinner. Outside a car comes to a screeching halt. Terrified they hold their breath. Who are they looking for? Are they coming for us? They freeze and sit motionless. Foot steps approach and halt in front of their door. They choke up. Then they hear banging on the front door.

"Open up!"

Should they or shouldn't they with Herman not being there. Worried, Mr. Gans decides to open the door. Two Dutch policemen enter uninvited. The one giving the orders speaks in a heavy Amsterdam accent.

"Kamphuis, go and take a look in the cellar." Kamphuis disappears into the cellar. The man in charge enters the living room, looks around and notices silverware on the table. He walks to the table and grabs the forks and knives. He wipes them clean on the white tablecloth and slides them into his coat pocket. He then moves over to the cupboard, opens a drawer, grabs another handful of silverware and slides it into his other pocket. Kamphuis returns from the cellar with a couple of home-canning jars. The boss nods and his partner lets the jars disappear into his pockets.

"Come on you, come along to the Theater."

"There must be a mix up. I work at the *Expo*. This is my husband." Sonja motions to her wedding photo.

"None of my business. They'll figure it out over there."

The three of them are escorted to the car and taken to the Theater. While their papers are being checked at the entrance, Sonja stops a young man from the Jewish Council and asks him if Herman is around. A few minutes later Herman comes rushing towards them.

"Wait here! Whatever you do, do not enter the auditorium. Once you're inside, they won't let you out."

Before she can tell him that Mr. and Mrs. Gans are with her, he disappears into the busy hallway. At the end of the hallway she sees him talking to someone. Moment's later, he returns with a young man in a German SS uniform.

"This is Günther. He is taking you home. Hurry. I'll see you later."

Günther escorts the three of them out of the building and drives them home in the same car that has brought them to the Theater no more than ten minutes earlier. In the car on the way home Mr. and Mrs. Gans make up their minds to go into hiding.

At home, Mrs. Gans hurries without delay to the bedroom and grabs the two backpacks. She tells Sonja they are going into hiding. She insists she comes with them, but Sonja refuses. Herman is still at work and she can't leave without him. They hug each other.

"Take good care of yourself."

Moments later Mr. and Mrs. Gans pull the front door shut and disappear from her life. She is alone. Fearful and jumpy at the slightest sound, she waits for Herman. When Herman finally comes home, she tells him that Mr. and Mrs. Gans have gone into hiding. He agrees that this address on the Apollolaan is not safe anymore. Friends in the Rijnstraat have a room for rent. The previous tenants have been deported and so Herman suggests they should go and stay there.

Sonja fills her backpack with a tube of toothpaste, a bottle of shampoo, her beloved photo album, several nice summer dresses sewed from her father's fabrics and postcards of the royal family that her father had sent her from his trips. With only two backpacks the move to the Rijnstraat is easy. Once in their new room Herman advises her to take her backpack to work in case she gets apprehended by mistake and they don't let her go home immediately.

1943

May 20. Aus der Fünten and Lages are longtime adversaries and argue over just about everything. In the beginning of May, Aus der Fünten leaves for a few days on a business trip to Germany. Herman continues working. The next big roundup is in Jonas Daniel Meijerplein. Lages decides to go and take a look for himself.

The phone rings at their new address in the Rijnstraat.

"There's a razzia on and around the Meijerplein. Jews with a *Sperr* are being detained." Herman sounds anxious.

"I'm going there to see if I can help. I'll be home late."

The Meijerplein is swamped with uniformed men: regular police, Dutch SS, German SS, Grüne Polizei, Green police so called because of their green uniforms. In reality they were the OrPo *(Ordnungs Polizei)* or order police. As soon as the victims see Herman they rush over to him. He doesn't want to attract attention and tries to calm them down. He gets his lists out, checks their names and tells them sympathetically, "I'll see what I can do."

Lages is watching from a distance. He sees the commotion and walks over, followed by several SS men.

"What's going on? What are you doing?"

Herman starts explaining that these people have been wrongly detained because they have a Sperr. Lages grabs the lists from Herman and while accusing him of sabotage he tears the lists up, without so much as looking at them. "Registering cases to bring them to the attention of the Germans was strictly prohibited. A young man working for the Jewish Council, who in May had tried it in the Meijerplein, was apprehended and immediately deported on a criminal prisoners transport." (H. Wielek, *De Oorlog die Hitler won*)

Herman hasn't come home. Sonja dies a thousand deaths. She is beside herself and stays awake all night. The following morning, earlier than usual, she goes to the *Expo*.

"Herman is in jail. Lages himself arrested him yesterday," Mr. Blüth tells her.

"They are keeping him at the Weteringsschans. That's all I know." She is desperate. She wants to go and see him but she herself might get arrested if she tries. Two weeks later Herman is deported to Camp Westerbork, where he is held in the punishment barracks, a barracks for criminals that had committed a crime as distinct from simply being Jewish. Aunt Bettie and her daughter Jennie are already at Camp Westerbork, as are Herman's two German uncles, Friedo and Jack. They have been there since 1938.

1943

June 20. It's an extremely warm Sunday morning, about ten thirty. There are rumors that security police, assisted by the *Grüne Polizei*, are rounding up Jews in Amsterdam-East. Sonja is in Amsterdam-South and reckons the roundups in Amsterdam-East won't affect her.

She hurries down the busy Noorderlijke Amstellaan, today the Roosevelt-laan, to the *Expo*. All of a sudden a passenger car screams into the street and comes to a screeching halt diagonally. Two men in SS uniforms and one in civil clothes jump out. A military truck enters the street from the far side, blocking off the street. The driver jumps out, keeping the engine of the truck running. About twenty policemen jump from the back, some are pulled by aggressive barking and teeth-showing Alsatians. The sudden sound of shrill whistles fills the otherwise peaceful neighborhood. Without realizing it, she is trapped in the middle of the last big roundup in Amsterdam. The policemen run up to anybody wearing a yellow star on their clothing. The SS men motion with their guns for the spectators to move on. One of the SS men sees Sonja's star on her coat. She is frantic. There's no way out.

"Papers," he barks at her.

She hands him her ID.

"Come along, get in."

Terrified of the uniforms, the guns and the barking dogs, she climbs into the back of the truck. About twenty men and women and a few children sit side-by-side on facing benches. One policeman climbs in, while the others disappear with their dogs around the corner. The driver drops the canvass cover and climbs behind the wheel. The passenger car with the SS men drives off. The street returns to being quiet and peaceful again.

The truck drives to a soccer field at Olympiaplein 15, in Amsterdam-South. At the entrance behind a row of tables, Jewish prisoners from Camp Westerbork are registering the new "load."

"ID! Address? Front door keys!"

She sees an acquaintance, a Council staff member, lugging suitcases and backpacks.

"Where are my parents? My little sister?"

He doesn't know. She asks him if he can pick her backpack up from the *Expo*. She gives him the key to the Rijnstraat room. She took her photo album out of her backpack and has forgotten to stick it back in. Half an hour later he returns with her backpack and her album. Quickly, under his breath, he tells her, "Your parents and Judie left for Camp Westerbork a couple of hours ago via the Polderweg station. You'll see them in Westerbork."

She thanks him for her belongings. He barely hears her. He's already busy with the next person. After being registered she is ordered to wait. She calms down somewhat. She sits down on the grass and contemplates. "I am going on a trip. Finally I will travel a bit. It's different from Zandvoort or Den Bosch. I am able to work." She searches through her backpack. She is pleased with her summer dresses and so happy with her photo album. She looks at Herman's photo for a split second. Yes, she almost feels relieved now. Herman is in Westerbork.

A few more hours and they'll be together again. To avoid creasing her dresses, she rolls them up more tightly. After waiting a couple of hours, they are ordered into the back of a truck. Packed together, no one says a word. At the Muiderpoort station they are beaten out of the truck. Surrounded by fifty or sixty people, some carrying only a backpack, others dragging a lot more of their belongings, she walks towards the train. A *Schalkhaarder* (a policeman specially trained in the village of Schalkhaar, to trace and capture Jews) walks next to her and whispers, "Girl, take off your star. Let me take you home. Don't be afraid. I will take care of you." She senses something is wrong.

"Is he talking to me?"

"Don't get into that train. Why do you wear that star? Tear it off."

"I am Jewish," she whispers back, looking at the ground ahead of her. He doesn't believe her.

"Take it off while you still can and come with me."

She had heard of several cases where people were rewarded money for reporting Jews. She thinks, "If I go with him, he'll report me to the police." He keeps insisting.

"Don't go. Come on, come with me."

"I am married, I am going to my husband in Westerbork."

"Take off your star," he whispers, "don't get into that train. You don't look Jewish. Listen to me!"

"I want to go to my husband."

She hesitates, "There is something you can do for me, if you really want to help."

"Whatever you want." She gives him her ration cards.

"Can you give this to my mother's neighbors, Van der Linden."

She tells him the address.

"Perhaps they can send me a care package now and then." He did deliver the ration cards as she had asked, for a few weeks later she did receive a care package during her stay in Westerbork. Years later Mr. Van der Linden tells her that the Schalkhaarder had said, "Too bad I couldn't change her mind."

The Nazis paid the Dutch Railways System with money they stole from Jewish bank accounts. Prices were fixed. For each Jew they paid a one-way ticket at fifty cents per kilometer, for the guards they paid one guilder for each return ticket. Trains ran to a tight schedule. Consequently the Dutch Railway System contributed to the extermination of the Jews in Holland. On June 20, 1943 six thousand Jews were deported in cattle cars to concentration camp Westerbork. It was dark and dirty inside the cattle cars. People were hungry. There was nothing to eat. Some were screaming. The stifling air was unbearable. Only one little opening provided fresh air.

She can hardly move. Children and babies are crying. More and more people are being pushed into her car; suitcases, backpacks, blankets. The car is packed. The heat is unbearable. She is sweating profusely. The door slides shut. She hears it being bolted. The locomotive with its fifteen cattle cars jolts and starts moving slowly. How did she get here? It doesn't add up. It all happened so fast. How did she end up in a cattle car on the way to Westerbork? There is no ventilation. Pressed together, they are gasping for air. Don't fall down, she thinks, or you'll get trampled. Her eyes adjust to the darkness. To a woman next to her she says, "At least the fear of being caught is gone. Tonight I can finally catch some sleep." The woman admits, "There's something to that." The sound of every click-clack brings her closer to Herman.

CONCENTRATION CAMP WESTERBORK

Concentration camp Westerbork, originally a refugee camp, came about in October 1939 when three thousand German Jews applied for political refugee status in Holland. The Dutch government declared, "If the Dutch Jews want us to let their German brethren in, they should pick up the tab for a camp." As a result Dutch Jews financed Westerbork. Preference for the location was the Veluwe, a desolate wooded area. The tourist bureau vehemently opposed the choice and Queen Wilhelmina made it known that she absolutely did not want a refugee camp within seven miles of her summer palace. The choice finally fell on an isolated plain near the village of Hooghalen, in the province of Drenthe, in the northeast of the country.

A small number of barracks were built. The first to arrive was a group of seven hundred and fifty German refugees. They were allowed to leave the camp for a few hours a day as long as they were back by nightfall. Due to all kinds of restrictions they couldn't help but feel like prisoners. Worse, they felt abandoned by the Dutch Jewish community.

"In the late thirties, the idea of a gated camp started to take shape and at long last the Dutch and German Jews were allowed to pay for their own concentration camp. The Dutch government didn't pay a penny." (Dick Houwaart, *Westerbork*)

Before it was completed, Westerbork started filling up with angry refugees. They were angry, because they were kept behind barbed wire in the middle of nowhere. They felt jailed more than ever. The required travel passes were almost impossible to come by. They blamed the Dutch Jews for not helping more, but the Dutch Jews found them ungrateful and reminded them that at least they were safe.

Hygiene was non-existent. There were fleas everywhere. Even in the washroom with its long row of faucets that ran the full length of the sink.

The camp quickly became a community. It established its own laundry facilities, bakery, hospital, etc. It even had its own camp currency. Gemmeker, the Nazi commander in charge, transformed Westerbork into a transit camp. Every Tuesday morning at 2 o'clock, the barrack leaders announced the names on the deportation list. In the morning at 11 o'clock, cattle cars were packed. Moments later the train left for an unknown destination in "the East." Once the train had left, artists performed a song and dance routine to distract the lucky ones that had remained behind. In

1945, when the camp was liberated, some nine hundred prisoners were left. Many of them had been betrayed, informed upon and had been apprehended at the address were they were hiding.

Concentration camp Westerbork is surrounded by ditches and barbed wire. SS guards have replaced the Dutch police and now man the seven watchtowers. In July 1942 the first train with 2000 Jews, including a group of orphans leaves for the East.

"The first trains ran in an unscheduled way, but as of February 1943 there was a regular timetable. Tuesdays were deportation days. The residents therefore lived from Tuesday to Tuesday." (H. Wielek, *De Oorlog die Hitler won*)

In 1939 the early residents of camp Westerbork were German and Austrian refugees, also known as the 'nobility' of Westerbork. Their mother language was German and obviously this worked to their advantage. They were the first to get acquainted with the camp's politics. They were put in charge of the day-to-day running of the camp. Personnel, barrack leaders, kitchen personnel, mailmen and cleaners, all needed to be scheduled, supervised and managed. The highest ranked of the early residents lived in small one and two bedroom cabins. They were issued travel passes on condition that they only visited relatives or friends and reported back before sundown. That's how things were until the Nazi invasion in May of 1940.

Fast forward to 1941. Now the Dutch Jews are starting to arrive. They want to work because they know that having a job can be a reason for getting your departure postponed. Jobs in the administration office, hospital or outside the camp working the fields, growing potatoes, rye, oats, wheat and beets, are the premium and most coveted jobs. However, these jobs are taken by the early residents; the same residents who remember that several years earlier their Dutch counterparts had made them feel neglected. Today the tables are turned. Now the early residents are "in charge." Herman's uncles Friedo and Jack are early residents. They have been living in Westerbork since 1939.

"Having a job gave some security. Working made the day go by more pleasantly. Nothing was worse than walking aimlessly through the muddy camp and wasting time desperately scheming how to get the coveted *Sperr* stamp. Just about everybody knew that those who were not employed were the first to get deported. You could take a class or play sports. Even shopping was possible. The camp used camp money in its 'store' or bar. There was even a moneychanger where you could exchange Dutch currency for camp money. For the children, life was not that unusual. There was a kindergarten and the older ones were required to take classes until the age of 15. This way life for the young camp residents continued pretty much as before. Lessons were often called off if the Tuesday train took too many teachers." (Westerbork website)

"They were given food during their lunch break and after work. There was a central camp kitchen. The food wasn't any good. Hygiene was worse, but the number of deaths compared to other camps, was not so high. Information index cards were kept inside the administration barracks. They were of vital importance. They mentioned every detail of every camp resident. One look at your card made your chances for deportation clear. Even though breaking the rules meant getting punished, life in camp Westerbork was reasonable. However bad it was behind barbed wire in Westerbork, at least you did not have to be scared of *razzias*." (S. van den Bergh, *Deportaties*)

"There were many surgeons, doctors, and dentists among the prisoners. Westerbork was extremely proud of its hospital. During the busiest times, the hospital counted over 1725 beds, 120 doctors and 1000 men and women personnel. Being sick in a barracks was not easy. On the plank-beds people lived and died, ate, were sick and sleepless. The horrible thing about Westerbork was the fear of being deported to places from where no word or sign of life was received. (S. van den Bergh, *Deportaties*)

"Turn in money and valuables you still have on you to Lippmann-Rosenthal bank agents." At their discretion they did let you keep a small amount.

Finally the locomotive with its long row of cattle cars comes to a juddering halt. Although Sonja feels tired and dirty, she can't wait to see Herman. The doors slide open. It's the middle of summer and it's dark outside. That means it must be late. Her thoughts are interrupted.

"Get out," it echoes along the endless row of cattle cars. Among slightly more than a thousand people she is herded into a big hall, the registration barrack, where they are ordered to wait. Soon the hall is filled to capacity and lines are formed outside. Inside grandmothers, grandfathers, aunts and uncles, parents, children, crying and sniveling babies, brothers, sisters, the sick and disabled, they all sit or lie on the floor amid their luggage waiting to be registered. Behind a long row of tables, Jewish prisoners are typing an information card for every arriving prisoner. Doctors hover about, checking on the exhausted elderly and children. It takes hours before it's Sonja's turn. While waiting, she sees Uncle Anton in the crowd rushing towards her. He greets her and tells her that he and Jet arrived a few weeks earlier and that he works in the hospital. He has no time to talk. He quickly tells her, "Your parents and little Judie arrived a few trains earlier. I admitted your mother and Mientje (his other sister) to the hospital. The beds are more comfortable than the bunk beds in the barracks. Hopefully my Judie and Hans are safe."

"What about Herman?"

He knows nothing about Herman and disappears into the chaos. Jacob's brother Nathan, his wife Janette and their two sons Jules and Sol arrived a month earlier, on the same day as Herman. Sol works at the administration office with the information cards. When a friend or relative is being sent on, Sol removes his or her index card. If a staff member inquires about the card, Sol says the card is probably misfiled. He tells them he is busy but that he will look for the card as soon as he has a moment. Once the transport has left, Sol puts the card back in its proper place and the friend or relative is assured of at least another week.

Sonja sees Sol hurrying about. She pushes her way through the multitude towards him. He is very busy but kisses her and tells her that her parents and sister arrived a little while ago.

"What about Herman? What do you know about Herman?"

He shakes his head apologetically and hurries to a typist who is calling him for help. When Sol sees the name of his uncle Jacob on the list of new arrivals, he tells his father that his brother Jacob has arrived. Nathan tells his other son Jules "Go and see if you can find your uncle Jacob and check if there's anything he needs." Jules goes looking for Jacob. When he finds him, he asks Jacob if he needs anything. Jacob answers, "I wouldn't know what. I'll be okay. With God's help we will all be fine."

Finally it's Sonja's turn.

"Name. Place of birth? Last address? Profession? Family?"

Moments later someone from the dwelling department barks, "Sonja Rosenstein, barrack 65!"

The triple-level bunk beds are so tightly packed together that they are only accessible from the narrow walkway that divides the barracks.

The new arrivals sprint for the bunk beds. Some prefer to sleep on top, others on the bottom. Sonja secures the top bunk, fourth from the door, not knowing that she won't be getting much sleep because the light in the corridor shines on her face all night.

She sits still for a moment taking it all in; the noise, the open suitcases, the clothes, the personal belongings everywhere. A young mother and her two children are dressed as if they are going on vacation.

"The barracks are best described as overpopulated storage facilities with changing inhabitants." (S. van den Bergh, *Deportaties*)

Her neighbor in the next bed fills her in on the rules and regulations of the camp. Be inside your barracks by 8 o'clock, in bed by 10 o'clock. Breakfast is a piece of bread and is at 8 o'clock. Sonja leaves her backpack on the bed and goes to the hospital in search of her mother, aunt Mientje and aunt Jet.

On the surface, the hospital seems chaotic. She first finds Aunt Jet. Jet tells her what happened in the town of Bussum, the town where she and Anton had been hiding. "We were betrayed for fifteen guilders, seven and a half guilders each. That is what the neighbor got, his reward for turning in two Jews. They took us to jail. A few days later Anton got caught trying to smuggle a note out of jail. When we arrived here, they first locked him up in the punishment barracks. A few days later they put him to work here in the hospital." Sonja hugs her and sadly asks if she knows where her mother is. She gratefully finds her mother in the chaos. They embrace. Her mother tells her how they were apprehended at home and given exactly two minutes to pack their bags. She even managed some last minute cleaning. While waiting for an army truck to take them to the train station, they watched a couple of men carry their piano down, load it onto a truck and drive away. Although Henrietta's foot operation was a success, she is happy to be in the hospital.

"There'll be plenty of walking later."

"What about father?"

"He is working."

"And little Judie?"

"Judie had a terrible train ride."

Sonja goes searching for her sister and finds her gasping on the floor of a dirty barracks. She is fighting an asthma attack. Several days later Anton succeeds in getting little Judie admitted to the hospital.

Either uncle Friedo or Jack arranges a job for Herman's cousin Jennie in the administration office. Herman is kept in solitary confinement in punishment barracks 67. His head is shaved and he is only allowed outside when accompanied by a guard.

"He performs heavy work. He starts early morning and gets little food." (H. Wielek, *De oorlog die Hitler won*)

Three weeks after Sonja's arrival, Jennie gets Herman admitted into the hospital. Finally Sonja gets to spend time with him.

Uncle Friedo works in the kitchen and being an early resident he gets Sonja a bread-buttering job. Now and then she hands a piece of bread to a hungry cousin. When she sees kitchen personnel stealing food, she protests. She gets transferred to the cleaning service. Every morning from seven to ten o'clock she mops the cabins of the early residents. The rest of the day she spends in the hospital with Herman, her mother, Jet and little Judie. A few weeks later Herman is diagnosed as "healthy" and is allowed to stay at the cabin with his uncles. Sonja and Herman spend their quiet moments together. Quiet moments before the storm; they are still unaware of how the next chapter of their life's program is going to play out. On her way to the hospital she runs into her father. He is pushing a wheelbarrow. He has lost weight and looks sick. She cries as she runs up to him.

"You don't need to cry. God helps us here, and God helps us there," he consoles her, "I can accept it."

Camp commander Gemmeker received the total number of Jews to be deported, by telex or telephone from Amsterdam. He left the choice of who was going to be deported up to the committee of early residents. Up until the fatal morning, it could be anyone's turn.

The committee met every Monday. They discussed schedules, responsibilities and logistics such as who and how many people go in which cattle car, car representatives and which doctors were to accompany the transport. After their meeting they would type up the infamous lists. No one outside the committee knew whose name was going to be read from the list. An empty train would arrive late on Monday night to pick up its new "cargo" on Tuesday morning.

"That night hardly anybody slept. People were packing. Early morning those about to be deported stood ready with all their belongings lined up in a row inside their barracks. The Jewish guards fetched people from barracks after barracks and drove them along to the platform." (S. van den Bergh, Deportaties) Those who stayed behind could breathe again for another week. It was especially horrendous for families that became separated.

There is not an empty bed left. Sonja sees her cousin Sara enter. Sara's parents Elie and Jette (Jette was Jacob's sister) had not really stayed in touch with Jacob and Henrietta all that much, consequently, the cousins had not either. Sonja calls Sara's name. Sara makes her way through the commotion towards Sonja. They embrace. Sonja insists that Sara shares her bunk. They spend fourteen days together. Then Sara's name is read. That Tuesday morning, with her pack on her back and ready to go, Sara says, "We won't ever forget these last days, eh, Sonja? Even if our parents haven't seen much of each other, when all this is over, we will catch up." They kiss and she is gone. Three days later Sara is dead, destroyed like vermin.

Sonja's all-time favorite book since elementary school is, "The Clog Maker and the Princess." Obsessed with the story, she wants the book for her birthday. But her parents don't discuss birthday presents. Birthday presents remained a surprise. How happy she had felt when she opened her present and looked eye-to-eye with the Princess! In short the story goes like this: The Princess can't find a pair of shoes that fit. The king holds a competition. Whoever makes the shoes that will fit his daughter's feet, will be well rewarded. A poor forester makes a pair of wooden shoes. The front of the clogs were painted to look like a dwarf's beard. The dwarf was painted wearing a red cap. The forester went to the palace. The clogs fit and the forester ended up a wealthy man. She must have read the book a hundred times.

Winters in Westerbork are muddy affairs. Sonja brought a pair of pretty pumps from Amsterdam but she can't wear them in the mud. She asks a carpenter to make her a pair of wooden shoes and tells him about "The Clog Maker and the Princess." She describes the clogs in detail.

"Can he make her clogs like the ones in the story?" A few days later she picks up a pair of lemon yellow clogs with a dwarf and a white beard painted on it. She feels a pang of bittersweet emotions.

She visits the hospital every day. A week after she arrives, Anton warns her that they are on to him. He can't keep her mother and little Judie in the hospital any longer.

"Our time has come. Father and I are leaving tomorrow. Little Judie is too," her mother tells Sonja on Monday June 28, 1943. She kisses her mother, returns at least twenty more times to give her that one last kiss.

1943

June 29. The following morning, her father, her mother, her sister Judie and her aunt Mientje are deported like cattle led to slaughter.

"Only six years earlier there had been a court case in Amsterdam against a cattle dealer who transported fifteen cows instead of fourteen in identical cattle cars, from the city of Zutphen to Amsterdam." (WW2 Westerbork website)

"Depending on the destination, the journey takes several days and nights. With all sorts of delays, resulting from bombs attacks, artillery fire and increasing chaos, it often took longer. It happened that a train packed with Jews waited in a station for weeks. The smell was unbearable. The Nazis knew an average of 3.6 Jews per square meter could be transported. People got sick

and died. The worst was the lack of water, especially for the little children."
(J. Presser, *Nacht der Girondijnen*)

She will never forget the shrill sound of the train's whistle. All of a sudden
they are gone. Not one of the nearly 2400 Jews, who leave that day, survives.

Thanks to the Nazis' excellent record keeping, we know many years later,
that on this particular Tuesday morning, exactly two thousand three hundred and
ninety seven mothers, fathers, uncles, aunts, sons, daughters, nieces, nephews and
cousins are deported to be gassed as soon as they arrive in a concentration camp
called Sobibor.

"Mother and father and little Judie are gone," it keeps flashing through her
mind, "but I still have Herman." She shivers.

"What does God still have in store for us?"

There are rumors that deported Jews are being murdered. She asks uncle
Jack if all those people on the train are going to be killed.

"My dear, please, how can that be possible? It can't be. Don't believe everything you hear. It's all propaganda."

Rumor has it that Theresienstadt isn't so bad. But Sobibor? She has to
throw up.

1943

*August. A criminal prisoner (someone who has actually committed a crime
as distinct from simply being a Jew) had escaped. Lages traveled to Westerbork to
investigate. As retribution he decided all criminal-prisoners were to be deported. If
Lages found out that Herman Rosenstein, the young man he personally arrested some
months earlier was still in Westerbork, he would have deported him immediately
to Auschwitz. Herman's cousin Jennie tried her best to get Herman's name on the
next Theresienstadt list. The Jews in Westerbork believed Theresienstadt was a better
camp than Auschwitz. But However, Lages did find out. He noticed Herman's name*

listed as still being a camp resident. What was Aus der Funten's protégé still doing here? Lages was furious and wanted Herman to be put on the train to Auschwitz the following morning. Early the next day Lages returned to Amsterdam, thinking that Herman was on his way to Auschwitz.

Thursday morning, August 12 was a hot summer morning. At 10:30 the mostly German-Jewish KaPo's, the camp police, (not an enviable job in hindsight) wearing brown uniforms, were working up a sweat. They were loading backpacks, suitcases and other personal possessions into about eighty filthy cattle cars. With barking dogs and SS men shouting, babies, children, parents and grandparents were loaded into boxcars.

Sonja and Herman have been married for exactly one year to the day. Their backpacks are loaded onto the train. They are the last to climb aboard. *KaPo's* are rushing alongside the train, chalking the number of persons in each car on the doors.

Cramped, sitting on the bare floorboards, without water or toilet facilities, only a bucket in the corner, they are on their way to Auschwitz. It's hot. Kids and babies are crying. Adults are screaming that they can't breathe. The ramp, an hour earlier a madhouse, is calm now. On the platform lists are checked and double-checked in typical German orderly fashion. The doors of the cattle cars are being bolted. It's their turn to climb in. My God! Is that door even going to close? Herman's uncles are crying in the distance as they watch them disappear behind the sliding door. They manage to close and secure the door. Suddenly approaching from the far end of the platform voices are heard yelling "Herman and Sara Rosenstein! Herman and Sara Rosenstein."

Staff members are running past the cars trying to locate them.

"Herman and Sonja Rosenstein! Herman and Sonja Rosenstein! In which car are you?"

"Over here!"

"Oh God," someone behind them moans, "they are getting out."

"Herman and Sonja Rosenstein!"

"We're over here!"

They hear the door unbolt. It slides open a tiny bit. A young camp policeman stands on the platform holding a list.

"Herman Rosenstein."

"Yes."

"You and your wife come with me. Quickly!"

They could barely make it out sideways. As she jumps out she remembers her backpack. She turns around but the door is already closed.

"My clothes! My photo album! Our wedding photos!" Herman squeezes her hand and guides her away from the train. Jennie waits for them inside the administration barrack. She cries as she hugs them. She explains Gemmeker and Lages had an argument and Herman's fate had inadvertently become a matter of prestige. Wanting to show he is in charge, Gemmeker ordered them off the train.

"You can't stay here any longer."

Jennie suggests Theresienstadt. Gemmeker agrees.

From his uncles' cabin they hear "their" train leave. They are safe, for now. Perhaps the war will be over by the time they leave. At least they have each other.

A few days later Gerdi and Emile arrive at Westerbork. Their parents have successfully bought Honduran passports and as a result they are now considered Honduran nationals. Hitler exchanges Honduran nationals for German prisoners of war and permits Honduran nationals to enter Switzerland by way of concentration camp Theresienstadt. Jacob and Henrietta could have afforded to do the same, but Henrietta had been afraid.

Jewish guards pushed wheelbarrows full of luggage to the train. After loading the luggage they took the wheelbarrows back to the barracks to transport the sick, disabled and elderly to the train.

Rabbi de Hond's name is read out. "Have I thanked him enough? After all it was Rabbi de Hond who had made sure that Herman and I were allowed to marry." She had known Rabbi de Hond her whole life. He had always been there for her. All of a sudden he disappears from her life. His wife Betsie, their four children, they all are being sent on. She makes sure to be at the platform on time to say 'good-bye.' Reconciled he smiles when he sees her approach through the commotion. He places his hands on her head and blesses her one last time. Dear Rabbi de Hond. Two days later he and his family are dead.

"It was a terrible journey. We had nothing. We stood, sat or lay in a cattle-train, all pressed against each other. There was a barrel in the corner for our bodily needs. I can still hear the rumbling wheels, smell the rotten stench, see all those desperate, frightened faces and feel the proximity of death."

(Fred Daniëls, *Endless Memories*)

"A sudden jolt of the train, and many of us fell down helplessly. People were moaning, wailing and weeping. Dutch soil, which had safeguarded the Jews for centuries, was moving mercilessly from under us…the overpowering stench coming from the so-called toilet. At first everyone tried to hold back, ashamed of relieving themselves in public, but soon indifference prevailed."

(Fred Daniëls, *Endless Memories*)

1944

February 25. Six o'clock in the morning. The weather is terribly cold. Against the rules, they wake up together in the cabin. An old run down passenger train to Theresienstadt is scheduled to leave at 11 o'clock. Sonja is nervous.

Herman tries to set her at ease.

"Everything's going to be all right." She has a hard time believing him.

"I'll be fine as long as they allow us to stay together."

She kisses him and goes to her room to fetch her belongings. She doesn't own much. One friend had given her a dress. From another she had got a sweater. She says goodbye to Jennie. Jennie's mother, her brother Alphons and his wife Frederique have gone. Now with Herman and Sonja leaving, Jennie only has her two uncles left. Come September and the three of them would be deported to Auschwitz.

Eleven o'clock. The train is packed with nine hundred and eleven individuals aboard. They are crammed with forty in a car designed for twenty-four. Before the train starts moving, the toilets are already filthy. She sits on Herman's lap. Gemmeker rides his bike along the length of the train. When he motions abruptly with his hand, they hear the wheels screech and the train jolts into motion.

Suddenly there are yelling voices coming from the platform. "What's that yelling?" Sonja almost faints.

"Are they calling us…? No, that can't be true."

That moment the engine driver sounds the ominous whistle. The train rolls slowly out of Camp Westerbork. At least she is with Herman. She leans back, her head on his shoulder.

Where are my parents, my sister, her uncles, aunts and cousins?" She dozes off.

In July 1944 two reports written by Auschwitz escapees were delivered to the Allied governments in London and Washington. The reports included detailed accounts of the murder actions going on in Auschwitz Birkenau: the number of transports, layout of the camp, sketches of the gas chambers, etc. These reports led to outcries to bomb the camp and the railways to the camp, but it is generally believed that the British Government and the United States War department rejected the

ideas because of technical, or rather political problems. The official explanation was
that a diversion of substantial resources was unacceptable.

Sonja and Herman belong to the four thousand five hundred and ninety seven privileged Jews from Holland for whom "the East" means Theresienstadt, for now. After three days and nights, the train arrives in Theresienstadt.

CHRONOLOGY ANTI-JEWISH MEASURES

1940

10 May: Nazi Germany invades Holland.

15 May: Holland capitulates

01 July: Jews are to resign from the civil air-raid protection services.

06 September: Jews are no longer appointed to public office. Those in office are not promoted.

26 September: Jewish newspapers shut down, except the Jewish Weekly.

05 October: All civil servants must sign a Declaration of Aryan descent, declaring their ethnic origin.

22 October: Jewish owned businesses are to be registered.

21 November: Jewish civil servants fired.

19 December: Jews prohibited from employing German domestic staff.

1941

09 January: It's against the law for Jews to enter movie theaters.

10 January: All persons with at least one Jewish grandparent must register.

12 February: The Jewish district in Amsterdam is signed Jewish Quarter. It is enclosed with barbed wire. Barricades are removed but signs remain.

13 February: The Jewish Council is set up in Amsterdam.

22 February: Over two days a total of 425 Jewish men ages 18 to 35 are arrested and deported to concentration camp Mauthausen.

25 February: The February Strike protests against the treatment of Jews.

15 April: Jews prohibited having a radio.

01 May: Jewish lawyers and doctors prohibited to have non-Jewish clients and patients. Jews prohibited from attending public markets.

31 May: Jews prohibited from using public swimming baths and public beaches.

11 June: Deportation of 300 Jews from Amsterdam to Mauthausen.

08 August: Jews are to transfer their money to a fictitious branch of the Lippmann-Rosenthal Bank.

1 September: Jewish children ordered to go to special 'Jewish' schools.

14 September: In the east of Holland, a hundred Jewish men are arrested and deported.

15 September: It's illegal for Jews to visit public parks, zoos, cafés, restaurants, hotels, theaters and museums.

07-08 October: One hundred Jews deported.

1942

09 January: Identity Cards for Jews have the letter 'J' stamped on them. Camps are set up for Jews.

20 March: Jews are prohibited from owning and driving vehicles.

25 March: Jews forbidden to marry non-Jews.

03 May: Jews age six and older must attach a yellow Star to their clothes, prominently displaying the word 'Jew.'

12 June: Jews may only shop at specific stores between 2 p.m. and 4 p.m.

30 June: Jews must remain inside between 8 p.m. and 6 a.m.

06 July: Jews are prohibited from using telephones and from visiting non-Jews.

14 July: First Jews are transported from Amsterdam to camp Westerbork.

15 July: 1,135 Jews are deported from camp Westerbork in Holland to death camp Auschwitz in Poland. Every week until 13 September 1944 cattle cars carry Jews from Westerbork to death camps in the Third Reich.

August: Jews are held in the Hollandsche Schouwburg, until they are deported.

02-03 October: Jews from other Dutch camps are taken to camp Westerbork and from there deported together with their families. Across the street from the Hollandsche Schouwburg, Jewish children are separated from their parents and await deportation.

1943

16 January: 450 Jews are transferred from the Hollandsche Schouwburg to the newly created concentration camp in Vught. A total of 12,000 Jews are imprisoned in camp Vught.

2 March: First group of Dutch Jews deported to extermination camp Sobibor.

10 April: Jews are forbidden to be outside of Amsterdam.

06-07 June: Children transports from camp Vught to concentration camp Sobibor.

29 September: Remaining Jews in Amsterdam are deported to camp Westerbork

19 November: The Hollandsche Schouwburg is closed after the last Jews are deported. Jews are deported to Theresienstadt.

1944

11 January: Jews are deported Bergen-Belsen.

02 June: Last transport of Jews from camp Vught to Auschwitz.

05-06 September: Allied forces reach camp Vught, right after all remaining prisoners are deported and the Nazis have abandoned the camp.

13 September: Final transports leave Westerbork for death camps Ravenbruck and Sachsenhausen.

1945

12 April: Westerbork is liberated. Nine hundred prisoners are alive.

Jacob & Henrietta get married February 1, 1922

Sonja, 1924

Pension Hiegentlich Zandvoort

Sonja, 1926

Sonja & Judie

Sonja & Judie

Zandvoort, 1931

Family Cohen, 1933
Sonja, Jacob (standing),
Judie, Henrietta

Sonja in 1937, 15 years old

Little Judie in 1937, 11 years old

Next to Herman Marga Grunberg

(Text: "Yours Forever")

Sonja & Herman, 1938

Sonja, 1940

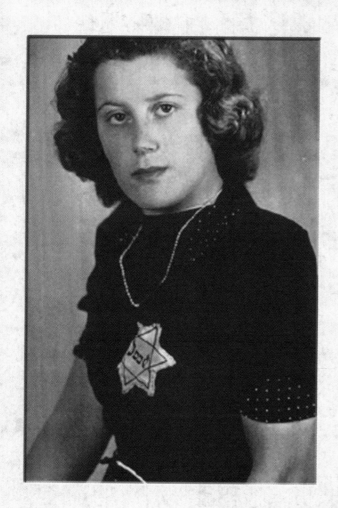 

Sonja (left) & little Judie
in 1943, weeks before their deportation.

BEWIJS VAN AANMELDING,

als bedoeld in artikel 9, eerste lid, van de Verordening No. 6/1941 van den Rijkscommissaris voor het bezette Nederlandsche gebied, betreffende den aanmeldingsplicht van personen van geheel of gedeeltelijk joodschen bloede.

JOODSCHE RAAD VOOR AMSTERDAM

De ondergeteekende, ambtenaar voor de aanmelding, verklaart dat de aan keerzijde aangeduide persoon, opgenomen in het Bevolkingsregister dezer gemeente, heeft voldaan aan de verplichting tot aanmelding volgens de bovengenoemde Verordening.

Afgegeven op _____ **- 9 APR. 1941**

in Gemeente _____ **AMSTERDAM**

voor den Burgemeester,
De Administrateur
afd. Bev.register en Verkiezingen,

Proof of Registration

Star of David to be attached to exact specified location on three layers of clothing.

BEKENDMAKING.

De Burgemeester van Soest brengt ter openbare kennis dat de Commissaris der provincie Utrecht van den Procureur-Generaal bij het Gerechtshof te Amsterdam bericht heeft ontvangen, dat onder „andere dergelijke plaatsen" als bedoeld bij paragraaf 1, onder b, der ambtelijke bekendmaking van den Hoogeren SS- en Politieleider, toegevoegd aan den Rijkscommissaris voor het bezette Nederlandsche gebied, ook de gemeente Soest wordt gerekend, zoodat aan in deze gemeente verblijvende

JODEN,

in den zin van paragraaf 4 der Verordening van den Rijkscommissaris No. 189 van 1940,

VERBODEN wordt het huren van kamers in publieke logeergelegenheden

(hotels, pensions, logementen).

Voor zoover eventueel aan dergelijke Joden door den Commissaris der provincie Utrecht vergunning is verleend in de gemeente Soest te verblijven, worden bedoelde vergunningen met ingang van heden ingetrokken.

SOEST, 20 Juni 1941.

De Burgemeester van Soest,
A. L. DES TOMBE.

Above reads: "Announcement. Rentals to Jews in hotels, pensions and beds and breakfast is AGAINST the law." Signed by the Mayor, The City of Soest

Zentralstelle für jüdische
Auswanderung Amsterdam
Adama v. Scheltemaplein 1
Telefoon 97001

N⁰ 124388

OPROEPING!

Aan ~~Marianne V. d. Kar~~
~~Th. Schwarzeplein~~ 5 hs
Amsterdam   t 280   No.

U moet zich voor eventueele deelname aan een, onder politietoezichtstaande, werk-
verruiming in Duitschland voor persoonsonderzoek en geneeskundige keuring naar het door-
gangskamp Westerbork, station Hooghalen, begeven

Daartoe moet U op _____ om _____ uur

op de verzamelplaats _____ aanwezig zijn

Als bagage mag medegenomen worden:

    1   koffer of rugzak
    1   paar werklaarzen
    2   paar sokken
    2   onderbroeken
    2   hemden
    1   werkpak
    2   wollen dekens
    2   stel beddengoed (overtrek met laken)
    1   eetnap
    1   drinkbeker
    1   lepel en
    1   pullover
        handdoek en toiletartikelen

en eveneens marschproviand voor 3 dagen en alle aan U uitgereikte distributiekaarten met
inbegrip van de distributiestamkaart.

De mee te nemen bagage moet in gedeelten gepakt worden.

a.   **Noodzakelijke reisbehoeften**
daartoe behooren: 2 dekens, 1 stel beddegoed, levensmiddelen voor 3 dagen, toiletgerei,
etensbord, eetbestek, drinkbeker,

b.   **Groote bagage**
De onder b. vermelde bagage moet worden gepakt in een stevige koffer of rugzak,
welke op duidelijke wijze voorzien moet zijn van **naam, voornamen, geboortedatum**
en het woord „Holland".
Gezinsbagage is niet toegestaan.
Het voorgaande moet nauwkeurig in acht genomen worden, daar de groote bagage in
de plaats van vertrek afzonderlijk ingeladen wordt.
De verschillende bewijs- en persoonspapieren en distributiekaarten met inbegrip van
de distributiestamkaart mogen **niet bij de bagage verpakt worden**, doch moeten,
voor onmiddellijk vertoon gereed, medegedragen worden
De woning moet ordelijk achtergelaten en afgesloten worden, de huissleutels moeten
worden medegenomen.

Niet medegenomen mogen worden: levend huisraad.   ←

Summons stating what to bring.
Arrow indicates text: "Don't bring 'live' property,'"
meaning animals.

Voor Joden verboden

DE PROCUREUR-GENERAAL
FUNGEEREND GEWESTELIJK
DIRECTEUR VAN POLITIE
VAN GENECHTEN

Reads: "No Jews Allowed"

Reads:
"During market hours
No Jews Allowed"

Left to Right: Gerti & Emile, Sonja & Herman, 1942

Jacob Cohen, 1942

The Journey

THERESIENSTADT

In Bohemia, in what used to be Czechoslovakia, about forty miles Northwest of the capital city of Prague, lies the former army fortress of Terezin. The Austrian Emperor Jozef II built the fortress to protect his territory during the 1790 Austrian-Prussian war. Josef II named the fortress after his mother, Maria Theresa. The complete fortification comprised of a bigger and a smaller fortress. The smaller fortress housed soldiers and political prisoners.

The bigger fortress was surrounded by thick walls and included ten garrisons strategically situated in a large circle. Each garrison was three stories high, contained windows overlooking an inner courtyard and was designed with straight streets and high, wide arches. The individual garrisons were so big that they were almost fortresses themselves. Each garrison had a name.

The Nazis changed the Czech name of Terezin, to the German name of Theresienstadt. They turned the big fortress into a concentration camp and kept the small fortress as a prison. Concentration camp Theresienstadt became a transit camp, comparable in that regard with Westerbork.

At the beginning of 1942 the original Czech inhabitants who called Terezin home, were evacuated and Theresienstadt became a ghetto. To be sent to Theresienstadt was considered a privilege. The Nazis used the camp in a propaganda campaign to show the world that Jews in camps had nothing to complain about. Originally the camp could hold six thousand people, meaning that's the number of beds it held. By the end of 1943 it housed fifty eight thousand. Overpopulation had its consequences. Lice and *typhoid were a daily problem. Toilets were filthy. There was no water or toilet paper. Taking a shower cost money. Washing just about belonged to the past. Delousing crews sprayed regularly, but that didn't help. Only after the war did it become known that every month thousands of prisoners had died, mostly of starvation, disease and the filthy conditions.*

There were several shops. There was one café with surrogate coffee, payable with ghetto money. "The shops sold possessions that the Nazis had stolen from the prisoners upon their arrival." (George E. Berkley, Theresienstadt)

At first there was a strict camp hierarchy. Here too, Nazi strategy put Jews in charge of Jews. The Westerbork Jews soon discovered that in Theresienstadt the Czech Jews were in charge.

In 1944, the very worst situation in the camp had peaked. Only a year earlier Theresienstadt had been bursting at the seams with German and Austrian Jews. Anywhere, from the unventilated attics with their spiders and rats, to the unpaved cellar floors covered with mattresses and clothes, newly arrived prisoners tried to find a space to lie down and call their own. Thousands of lives connected during a moment of chaos.

The railway from the station of Bauschowitz had been extended to the entrance of the camp by the time Herman and Sonja arrived. Before the extension and after their horrendous train ride, the dehydrated and starved victims had to lug their belongings two miles to the camp. Flanked by Czech guards, they walked in rows of four to the entrance of the camp. Some of the guards acted more or less compassionately; others beat elderly people and parents carrying children for not moving fast enough.

The unsuspecting travelers were taken to the registration center and ordered to fill out forms asking about their education and work experience. Next, all remaining valuables, even sanitary napkins, were seized, never to be returned. Just as in Westerbork, they were advised to hide nothing. Unlike Westerbork though, they were not allowed to keep even the smallest amount of money. Women were ordered to undress for physical inspections.

The KaPo's, the camp police, were mostly political and heavy criminal prisoners. They were in charge of the work details. They needed to show the SS that they were ready and able to beat up, kick and club the prisoners without mercy or they themselves stood to get a good thrashing from the SS. The murderers and rapists were only too eager to oblige.

"Their living situation was abominable. Because better housing in the ghetto was occupied by the time they arrived, they were assigned to the Hamburger barracks. There they slept closely together, on filthy straw bags…they received no packages from home…" (George E. Berkley, *Theresienstadt*)

Sonja and Herman are taken to the Hamburger barracks where they join other Dutch nationals. Sonja lands in room 112. It is a room with twelve double bunk beds for 24 Czech women. A woman in the room informs her in German about the rules of the camp: the hierarchy, sporadic water, not enough food, whom to trust, whom to stay away from, what is allowed and what isn't. Someone tells her that work detail Kader Hundertschaft is bearable. The following day Sonja registers with that detail. They give her a blouse and a pair of dark brown overalls and they put her to work with ten men and women. Every ten days her group gets a different assignment. First they work ten days in the hospital, and then they switch to ten days of cleaning offices, after that they work ten days in an elderly home and ten days in the bakery, etc. Everyone wants to work in the bakery because Theresienstadt means going hungry.

The day starts at six a.m. In a large washroom with a long basin and a hundred faucets, they consider themselves lucky if they get a couple of drops of cold water.

The bakery detail starts at seven o'clock. She learns how to knead bread, how much hot water is needed to spray on the loaves to make them shiny, how to place the loaves in the oven and when to take them out. Afterwards she drops the loaves off at the distribution windows throughout the fortress. At the end of the day she often smiles at the Czech baker. He will nod at her, meaning she can go ahead and take the leftover pieces of bread. It goes without saying that all this is done discreetly. Getting caught means deportation to Auschwitz.

During one of her shifts she gets her hands on a small bag of flour. She is hoping to make pancakes on the stove in her room. When her shift is over she hides the bag in her underpants. On the way to her building the bag starts to leak. Unaware she leaves a Hans and Gretchen type trail. The girls behind her warn her. She pretends suddenly to experience stinging pains in her side. The girls lace their fingers together and make her a seat to carry her back. The tiny pancakes are delicious.

Herman works in the agriculture detail. His hours are from seven in the morning to six in the evening. He grows miniature potatoes and cauliflowers, strawberries, apples, pears and cherries on a piece of land outside the camp. Everything the prisoners grow is only for the Germans.

Herman is in good condition. He works hard and looks healthy. The men in his work detail like him. So do the German guards. Like all young married women, when she gets the chance, Sonja sneaks off to visit Herman in his room, one floor up. She brings him bread and anything else she manages to get her hands on.

When he is still at work and she is finished for the day, she goes to the spot where she can observe his detail walking back into the camp. She feels the piece of bread in her pocket she is saving for him. She is tired and dozes off. In her dream she sees her father, arriving home from *shul*. Her mother cuts him a piece of gingerbread. She pretends to be late for school so she can go and meet Herman. She kisses her father hastily. She doesn't dare to look her mother in the eye. Her mother knows about Herman. Boy, that food on the table sure looks good!

The sound of marching footsteps wakes her. Herman's detail marches by. Herman isn't with them. She freezes. Where is he? What's wrong?

"He's in jail," one of the men in his detail tells her.

"He sowed the sleeves of his jacket shut and filled them up with vegetables. One of the guards noticed his sleeves dangling."

She is beside herself with fear. She goes looking for Jo Spier, the well-known 43-year-old Dutch water colorist who is well connected because the Nazis like his paintings. When she finally finds him, she tells him what has happened. A few days later Herman is let out of jail.

"When we are back in Amsterdam, I have to tell you something important," Herman tells her that same evening.

"Why not tell me now?"

"Once this is all behind us and we are back in Amsterdam."

She doesn't insist. Many years later she remembers telling aunt Bettie when looking at a photo of Herman's parents, "Herman doesn't look anything like his father."

"That's not his father," aunt Bettie had replied. She had not insisted then either.

"On May 15, 16 and 18, 1944 three transports left *Theresienstadt* with a total of seventy five hundred people of all ages: elderly, children, healthy young men and women, all going supposedly to an area near the city of Dresden." (George E. Berkley, *Theresienstadt*) In reality they were taken to Auschwitz where they were gassed a few hours after their arrival. Of the seven thousand five hundred people, five hundred were Dutch.

While Herman is in jail she tries to stay busy by welcoming trains arriving from Westerbork. The sight of a familiar face in the crowd gives her a momentary sense of happiness, even though after the three-day cattle car ride, the familiar faces are far happier to see her than the other way around. Ben Meijer, a cousin of her mother's and a violinist with the Amsterdam Concertgebouw orchestra, steps off the train. Sonja shoots towards him. He notices she has lost weight.

"How is it here? You haven't been eating."

"It could be worse. Herman is here too. He's at work. He was in trouble but everything is okay now."

He shows her a photo of Mengelberg, the conductor of the Concertgebouw orchestra.

"I am on my way to Switzerland. Willem Mengelberg arranged for me to be sent here. If I get out of this mess alive, I will owe my life to him."

He goes through the registration routine and is assigned to a room. As she takes him to his building she tells him about the camp and her work and that there is very little to eat.

"I can tell you haven't been eating properly. Do you want a real Dutch sandwich?" He hands her a sandwich. She wolfs it down.

"Oh, this aged cheese is delicious," she says, loving every bite of it.

"That's not cheese," he explains, "That's probably the rancid butter from Westerbork. Listen, there's talk about an allied invasion. I think this war will soon be over."

"From your mouth to God's ears."

1944

Tuesday June 6. D-day. American and British troops landed on the west coast of France. For a while there were no deportations. The prisoners breathed slightly easier.

July 20. A failed assassination attempt was made on Hitler's life.

The center of the camp underwent a metamorphosis. Buildings were painted. Parks, playgrounds and cafés were constructed. Tablecloths and flowers in little vases decorated the café tables. Windows on the downstairs floor were beautified with flowerpots and curtains. Rumors spread like wildfire that on behalf of the international community, committee delegates of the International Red Cross were coming to pay the camp a visit. The Jewish orchestra conducted by Rafael Schächter started practicing Verdi's Requiem. Prisoners were given bigger food rations.

"The children received special attention…a playground was built, complete with sand boxes, kiddy baths, swings, rocking horses and other goodies. When the day approached that the delegation was to visit, the streets were cleaned, the sidewalk scrubbed with water and soap." (George E. Berkley, *Theresienstadt*)

Answers were rehearsed. Prisoners who refused to cooperate were locked up. Producer, director, actor Kurt Gerron, a celebrity who fled from Germany to Holland where the Nazis caught up with him all the same, was responsible for entertainment on that day. Gerron assembled a choir and started rehearsals.

Herman tells Kurt Gerron that Sonja has a beautiful coloratura soprano voice. Gerron rehearses the choir in the Maagdenburger barracks. Herman arranges a meeting between Gerron and Sonja during a quick rehearsal break in the stairwell. She tries to sing but her nerves are frazzled and her voice fails her.

"Go ahead, sing, you've got such a great voice," Herman encourages her. She clears her throat and tries again but it's no good. She can't sing a note. She apologizes. Herman thanks Gerron for his time. Walking back to their barracks he tries to cheer her up and tells her not to worry. He will be playing soccer that afternoon and his first goal will be for her. He can tell she's extremely disappointed but her inability to sing will later save her life.

1944

Friday, June 23. Maurice Rossel, a 26 year-old Swiss national and two Danish public officials visit a scene comparable to that on a movie set. Everything to the smallest detail has been taken care of. The prisoners are warned not to come too close to the three observers or they will face deportation. They still don't know what that means, but it sounds dreadful enough. Now and then a guard hands her a postcard that says that this or that friend is all right. "With me everything is fine. We are here all of us together pleasantly in …" But she doesn't put much faith in the cards she receives. She has had to write a card or two herself.

This one Friday though, they feel like normal people. They get a little more food than usual and they are allowed in the street. Maurice Rossel takes pictures and is under the impression that the prisoners in Theresienstadt have nothing to complain about. In his report he notes that the living conditions in Theresienstadt are reasonable and that nobody lacks for anything.

"Especially his closing paragraph is telling: …everybody has the right to condemn the point of view of the Reich on how to solve its Jewish problem… His reference to 'the Jewish problem' of the Reich only shows that he was everything but impartial. Only anti-Semites believed that the Reich had a Jewish problem." (George E. Berkley, *Theresienstadt*)

Immediately after Rossel's visit, Kurt Gerron, the orchestra and the choir for which Sonja tried out, are deported to Auschwitz and killed. Two weeks later another 11.000 prisoners are sent to the gas chambers.

1944

August 25. Paris was liberated. Everyone hoped that the war would be over soon. In Theresienstadt thousands of prisoners were dying from starvation and dehydration. Hard labor also took its toll. Theresienstadt remained a transit camp to the ovens of Auschwitz.

September. There are more rumors. An all-male transport will be leaving soon, heading toward the city of Dresden. (In actual fact there were three transports.)

"The men will be building a new labor camp, while the remaining wives and children will be well taken care of." (George E. Berkley, *Theresienstadt*)

Herman is ordered to leave for Dresden. Against camp rules they spend their last night together. Fortunately no one bothers to check. They say goodbye near the gate. Jimmy de Nijs, a friend from Holland is leaving too. Sonja is in total agony but tries to hide it.

"Make sure you stick together."

They kiss.

"See you soon." She tries not to cry.

"Somewhere we'll meet up. I can feel it right here." Placing her hand on his heart he tries to set her at ease.

"They will start evacuating the camp when the Americans get closer. When that happens, you must try to stay behind. I have a feeling it's better if you stay put. Wait for the Americans." She tells him.

"Stop worrying so much. Everything's going to be fine. I will see you back in Amsterdam or perhaps sooner." One last kiss and he and Jimmy are gone.

Like thousands before them, Herman and Jimmy were lied to. They didn't go to Dresden to build a labor camp. They were sent to Auschwitz. (It is known that one or two men in Theresienstadt survived by hiding in an attic of one of the many buildings until the camp was liberated.)

A few days later one last transport arrives from Holland. As Sonja prays to see a familiar face, Gerdi and Emile (now her husband) and his mother, get off the train. Thanks to their newly bought Honduran passports, they are on their way to Switzerland.

She hugs them warmly. She hears that Gerdi's parents have been sent via concentration camp Bergen Belsen to Switzerland, where days after his arrival, her father collapsed of a heart attack and died. Emile's father died in Amsterdam before they were deported. Emile asks about Herman.

"He's in Dresden, building a camp. I miss him so terribly. They promised though, we'll see our husbands again when they are done," she says naively.

On their way to register, she explains the rules and regulations. While waiting in a sandy gravel area amid the hundreds of people from their transport, Gerdi eyes the ground and asks if they are coming back to this waiting area later. Sonja doesn't understand the question but shakes her head.

"No."

Gerdi and Emile take one look around. Without being seen they quickly kneel down and start digging. Sonja is shocked. She had just finished explaining that hiding valuables means deportation. Within a blink of an eye, Gerdi and Emile stick a paper pouch holding several diamonds and a wad of cash into the ground, quickly covering it with earth. While stamping the sand, they study the location carefully.

"We have no choice," Emile explains, "It's all we have left when we get to Switzerland."

Only seconds later guards carrying machine guns herd them along into the registration area. Gerdi and Emile have nothing to declare. A few days later Emile surreptitiously returns to the location. He finds the spot and digs up his valuables.

Sonja is upset. She has got used to the Hamburger barracks. It's where she and Herman spent time. It's where she feels closest to him. Now she is ordered to find a sleeping spot in the Maagdenburger barracks. The upside is that Gerdi and Emile sleep in the Maagdenburger barracks. It's not a complicated move. She owns nothing. Her backpack and her photo album are gone. She misses her photo album terribly. The only thing she owns is the dress on her back. And even that is Gerdi's.

Rumors have it that all women whose husbands have been sent to Dresden need to report. "You are going to join your husbands," promises an SS captain. "Your husbands have been told you are coming." Thinking of Herman she believes the captain. It keeps her going.

We will probably have to work hard, but we are young and at least we will be together with our husbands. Not for a moment does she think she is being lied to. Finally, she is going to be with Herman. Her fear is somewhat lessened. She kisses Gerdi, Emile and his mother goodbye and wishes them good luck on their trip to Switzerland as she climbs, unbeknownst to her, into a train bound for Auschwitz. After the war she is told that Gerdi became very sick and that Emile and his mother decided not to abandon her. They intentionally missed the last train to Switzerland, to freedom, to take care of her.

It's the middle of the night. She boards the train with two thousand other women. Again she is somewhat relieved because she is going to Herman. Then an ominous feeling comes over her as rumors persist that the train is headed for Auschwitz.

What if these rumors are true?

She takes it all in.

How did I get here? It doesn't add up. It all happened so quickly. What if we are on our way to Auschwitz? What is this mysterious Auschwitz anyway?

She looks around. Her cousins Florrie and Sere, Stella and Jettie Cantor, the singer who immediately recognized Sonja's operatic voice, Mienie's mother, Mienie and her children, Saartje, Bettie, Reneetje, Helga's mother and Helga who is very pregnant.

What I wouldn't do to have my mother right here with me, she thinks to herself. Where are mother, father and little Judie?

Lientje announces that she's tired of working and wants to take it easy from now on. Like sardines in a can they are stuffed into a packed cattle car. Each car has two buckets; the first is filled with water, the second is empty to be used as a toilet. The first is immediately empty and the second is full in no time.

THE AUSCHWITZ COMPLEX

The town of Oswiecim in Poland lies approximately one hundred and forty miles southwest of the capital city of Warsaw on the river Sola. After the Germans invaded Poland in 1939, they changed the town's name to Auschwitz. A land climate produces hot summers and extremely cold winters. In 1914 Oswiecim had some ten thousand inhabitants of which half were Jewish.

"The authorities had built a camp with brick houses for migrants but in 1918 it was used as military barracks for the reconstructed Polish army." (van Pelt & Dwork, Auschwitz) Later it became a tobacco factory and after the German invasion it was turned into a concentration camp for Polish political prisoners. In 1941 Auschwitz 1, the administration center, was extended and the much larger camp of Birkenau was added. Death camp Birkenau and labor camp Monowitz, both satellite camps, were also called Auschwitz II and Auschwitz III. Death camp Birkenau was situated three kilometers North West of Auschwitz I and was surrounded by deep ditches, guard posts and 2000-volt barbed wire.

In 1942, after having used gas on smaller trial groups of Jews, the Nazis began to gas larger groups. Upon arrival some were registered, but the large majority was immediately gassed, without being registered. Until 1943 the bodies were thrown into mass graves. Not before all hair was shaved and golden teeth and fillings were extracted. (Their hair was collected and used for all sorts of diverse purposes; from felts in submarine crew shoes to mattresses for soldiers. The mouths of the dead were inspected for gold teeth and fillings and were pulled out by prisoners. The gold was melted and deposited in Nazi bank accounts. In all about four million Jews met their fate in Birkenau.)

During the course of 1943, the Nazis used the prisoners to build four gas chambers. To make the gassing process more efficient, the gas chambers were supplied with electric elevators that transported the dead bodies to the ovens (crematoria) where they were burnt. These ovens had the capacity to burn 4,000 bodies a day.

Prisoners selected to stay alive were shaved. Next they were ordered to undress in a changing room resembling the changing room of a swimming pool, including numbered hooks for clothes. The room looked spotless. Guards reminded them to: "Remember your number to find you clothes afterwards." They were told to tie their shoes laces together. Long-term prisoners walked about handing out soap and towels.

In several places there were signs saying, "Keep clean" and "Don't forget your soap."

Most religious Jews had never been naked in the company of strangers before, but welcoming a nice warm shower, they undressed. Naked children, elderly, sick, mothers with babies, all were driven into the shower room. A thick steel door, just like the door of a bank vault, sealed the room airtight. An SS man on the roof threw Zyclon-B gas capsules down through an opening in the roof. These capsules released cyanide gas. People started yelling, crying, begging to be let out, etc. Within half an hour everyone was dead. Occasionally a child on the floor beneath a pile of dead bodies survived because an air bubble had formed under the pile of bodies. Survivors were immediately shot.

DEATH CAMP BIRKENAU

After three days and three nights the train finally jolts to a stop. Sonja is famished and dehydrated. She has had no food or water since she left Theresienstadt. She is stiff and feels absolutely filthy. She is completely exhausted. Someone whispers that it must be around four in the afternoon. Outside they hear dogs barking, voices cursing, yelling and screaming. The bolted door of her car disengages and slides open. It is twilight. Bright searchlights are focused on the doors. SS soldiers pointing their guns at the vulnerable women are shouting, "*RAUS, RAUS*," while the women, closest to the door, are brutally beaten out of the car.

"Get out! Dirty rotten Jews! Out!"

The ferociously barking dogs make this supernatural spectacle complete. The SS men pull, kick and beat the unsuspecting women out of the train. The SS soldiers order their vicious dogs to attack.

"Quickly!" they scream in Polish and German.

"Get out! Quickly. Leave your stuff in the train."

The woman ahead of her is next. She jumps. The dogs bite at her feet. She sees the woman fall. She gets up and is kicked to the side. This time around the

KaPo's are Polish. They curse in Yiddish.

"Leave all luggage behind! Line up in rows of five! Leave all luggage in the train!"

Now it's her turn. She stands in the doorway. The sudden bright lights blind her eyes. It takes a moment to adjust to the dreadful racket. She is clubbed and dragged out of the car without understanding what is going on. Then she is brutally pushed to the side. They are ordered to form a line. She sees searchlights, barbed wire, barking dogs, hollering KaPo's, and cursing SS men. The picture presents an ominous setting. There's a foul pungent odor that she can't place. Gunshots sound nearby.

"This must be hell," she whispers to Saartje Stuiver. Watches and rings, valuables they have managed to hold on to until now, are now swiftly taken from them. Guards push and kick them into a line that moves towards several men sitting behind a table. (One of them could well be the infamous doctor Joseph Mengele, who tortures his victims in the name of science.) A woman in line ahead of her says, "They are asking if you are healthy and if you can work." The doctor motions the elderly, children under sixteen and all those obviously unable to work to the left. This so-called medical check, after the war known as "selection" is accompanied by kicking, clubbing, barking dogs and gunshots. It seems entirely unreal. Is this a bad dream and will she wake up in bed next to Herman? Mienie stands with her mother and her children in front of 'Mengele.' With a careless motion of his hand he waves Mienie to the right. He motions her mother and the children to the left. Mienie asks if she may join her mother and children.

"You'll see each other tonight," was his answer.

"See you later mama, take good care of the children," Mienie calls after her mother. Because of her wide coat it goes unnoticed that Helga Lipinski is very pregnant. She is sent to the right. So is her mother.

"I'm not going to tell them that I'm healthy," says Lientje, "I'm no fool.

I've worked hard enough in Theresienstadt. I want to save my energy." 'Mengele' puts her at ease in a friendly manner and assures her that she doesn't have to do a thing. He motions her to the left. While Sonja is wondering about the difference between left and right, she notices a woman behind barbed wire, dressed in black rags and a headscarf. She holds her hands out in front of her.

"What does she want?" Sonja whispers.

"She is asking for food," someone whispers. Again the woman holds out her hand.

"Food, food," she keeps crying out in Polish.

Suddenly they hear the sounds of a shot. The woman falls backwards. Sonja notices the woman is not wearing underwear.

"Oh my God, what is this place?" she says to herself.

It's her turn. She steps forward and stands eye to eye with 'Mengele.' She has no idea she is standing across from the most powerful man of Auschwitz. Head of all the doctors in the camp, better known as the "Angels of Death," who with a mere gesture of his hand or a snap of his finger, is responsible for the death of thousands of Jews. He pinches her cheek.

"Are you healthy?"

"Yes I am."

He sends her to the right. From the nearly two thousand women on her transport, only fifty or sixty are sent to the right and pass the selection. All the others have nonchalantly been sent to the left. She has no idea that an hour later the nineteen hundred and fifty women of her transport are dead.

They are ordered to walk. Escorted by guards and immensely aggressive dogs, about an hour later, they pass under the steel gate at the head entrance to Auschwitz I. The words *ARBEIT MACHT FREI* (work sets you free) adorn the top of the gate.

"That's what I've thought all along, we have to work." She lets out a sigh of relief. She is cold, dog-tired, hungry and nauseous.

AUSCHWITZ I

Sonja's group is taken to an enormous room, where they are ordered to undress. They stand in line naked, as their clothes are taken away. Several soldiers enter with razors and shave all their hair off: their head, their armpits, their legs and their pubic area. They do a quick and rough job and leave cuts and traces of blood on all of them. Helga, who is expecting a baby any moment, stands next to Sonja. A German doctor notices she is pregnant.

"What are you doing here?" He asks her politely. He calls a young guard.

"This young lady here is in the wrong place. Take her to where she belongs."

Helga's mother rushes to the front and asks if she may please join her daughter.

"Yes, of course you may."

He smiles well mannered. The guard takes both of them to the gas chamber.

Next, Sonja and her group are taken into a shower room and told to wait. Did they expect a strong warm stream of water after traveling three days in a cattle car without eating, drinking or toilet facilities? Saartje next to her says half jokingly, "There had better be water coming out of that." It trickles a few drops of icy water, but it's water. Naked and wet they are hunted out of the shower room, and into to a barracks crammed to the ceiling with rags. She sees a mountain of old and dirty clothes.

Someone keeps yelling, "Three pieces only! Take three pieces only and stand in line." They are cold and rush towards the rags. Those not fast enough are kicked and whipped. The guards constantly hurry them. Sonja gets hold of two worn left shoes that are too small and a torn thin see-through summer dress. Shivering she puts the dress on. A woman, who takes an extra shirt is beaten and drops the shirt. Sonja sees a flannel overall and remembers her bladder infections every winter. She quickly grabs it and puts it on underneath the thin dress. She snatches an old worn coat with a red cross on the back. Later she notices the others also have a cross on their back. Just like the more familiar pin striped black and white prison uniforms, a cross on the back identifies a prisoner and makes escaping more difficult. There's no time to search for anything better.

"Pieces of dirty underwear, tight short pants and jackets too small for any adult…in these clothes every human being looks like a clown from a traveling circus." (*Seweryna Szmaglewska, Rook Boven Birkenau*)

By now it is two o'clock in the morning. What are they going to do with us? She feels she has to throw up but her stomach is empty and she only brings up acid. They are beaten out of the barracks and ordered to stand in rows of ten. She starts to itch terribly. The clothes she is wearing are riddled with fleas. All of a sudden she is part of an enormous convoy comprising one thousand women, one hundred rows of ten. It seems too unreal. The guards in the watchtowers observe the one thousand heavily guarded women being escorted out of the camp. An hour later she drags herself exhausted and dispirited through the gates of Birkenau. It is three o'clock in the morning.

BIRKENAU

"There are no roads or paths between the barracks. In the whole camp there is no water or ducts. There is dirt, human excrement and trash, stinking and rotting, everywhere. No birds ever fly over Birkenau, although the prisoners keep searching the skies for them during their endless roll calls. Smell or instinct makes the birds avoid this place."(*Seweryna Szmaglewska, Rook Boven Birkenau*)

The camp is surrounded by 2000-volt barbed wire. Searchlights illuminate glimpses of rows of stone blockhouses and wooded barracks stretching endlessly ahead of her in a sea of mud. She is dead tired. She doesn't believe her eyes. She can't possibly comprehend it. She still smells that dirty pungent odor she can't place. When the thousand-women convoy wades past a smoking chimney of a crematorium, a woman in the outside row asks a German guard with his finger on the trigger, "What is that smell, that odor?"

"That's the bakery," he laughs. His answer spreads like wildfire.

"Do you hear that? That smell is the bakery. One of the guards says it's the bakery."

They believe him. Never would she forget the stench of burning flesh of dead bodies.

Birkenau consisted of a male and a female camp. Female KaPo's were in charge of the female camp and they in turn were responsible to the SS. Just as had been the case in Westerbork and Theresienstadt, the most sought-after jobs involved extra food and were mostly available through connections, which were built over time. The Polish women had been there the longest and consequently they had the most desirable jobs. They were responsible for law and order. They made sure that newly arrived prisoners kept the barracks and the toilets clean. The most senior of the Polish KaPo's had a whip. She knew the SS guards wanted to see her use it. In return for extra food, she needed to be whipping somebody constantly. If they thought she wasn't brutal enough, they would replace her.

Her group is forced into a wooden barracks. Passing a door to a tiny sleeping spot for the *KaPo*, she sees an enormous area filled with thousands of triple-level bunk beds. Three women sleep in one space or cage as they are called, even though there is only room for two. The bunk beds are touching, so that due to the cramped space, the third woman is pushed partially onto the "mattress" of the neighboring cage. The "mattresses" are jute bags filled with a little sand, gravel and straw and are placed on bare wooden floorboards. There are two wood-burning stoves in the middle of the aisle, but the only pieces of wood available are too wet to burn. Small groups of women stand around the stoves, talking.

Sonja, Sere and a third woman lie cramped on a top cage. Saartje, Stella and Mientje find a cage nearby. A cage is so tight that when one of them turns, the other two have to turn too. Sonja lies on the outside. When Mientje asks a Polish *KaPo* when she will get to see her mother and two children again, the *KaPo* snaps indifferently, "They are already up there."

"Up there?"

Surprised they look up and notice the barrack's wooden beams. They don't understand.

"Up where?"

Thinking the *KaPo* hasn't understood her question, Mienie asks her again. Once more the *KaPo* motions upward. Mienie realizes that her mother and children might be dead. She starts screaming. The Dutch women try to comfort her.

Day and night they wear the same dirty itchy rags. There is the continual sound of crying and screaming. On Sonja's first night there is a woman wailing throughout the night. Nobody pays any attention to her. Sonja wants to comfort her but some women discourage her. All the screaming, yelling and crying make it hard to sleep.

"It is unthinkable to fall asleep here. When the women lie down to sleep, from all nooks and crannies millions, billions of lice appear. Apart from the big ones, there are the small ones whose bites you feel. They fill up with blood in no time, so that their thin, skinny membrane explodes with the slightest touch. Blood stains and many tiny red spots remain." (*Seweryna Szmaglewska, Rook Boven Birkenau*) The first night she is terrified. Although she has diarrhea, she doesn't dare to leave her barracks to find the toilets.

Toilets were two non-partitioned rows of twenty holes in the ground and were filled to the top with human feces. Sitting above a hole, back to back, your feet in excrement, was a filthy affair; the stench was brutal. There was no toilet paper. There was shit everywhere. Everyone walked right through it; as a consequence many prisoners died of dysentery and typhoid.

Her stomach cramps are unbearable. She can't hold it in anymore. She takes a quick look around her. She has to go so badly. What can she use? Sere uses her wooden shoes as a pillow or they are sure to be stolen. But they had slipped out from under her head. Careful not to wake her, Sonja gets hold of Sere's clogs. She climbs down and craps nervously filling the first clog to the rim, than the second. Sere wakes up momentarily, but falls back asleep. During roll call a few hours later, Sere stands bare feet on the freezing cobblestones. She curses Sonja who confessed to being the culprit.

Sonja notices the woman who wailed all night, hanging from the barbed wire. The two thousand-volts barbed wires have killed her. Every night at least fifty or sixty women run purposely into the high-voltage wires.

Back in the barracks *KaPo's* hand out carton dishes with an aluminum spoon and a fork attached. It looks like a camping kit. The spoon is adorned with a small decorative swastika.

Losing your dish meant forfeiting your "soup." Soup in reality consisted of a watery substance with several inedible blades of grass, sand and pebbles, which the prisoners spit out. Every night the barracks-leader handed out the soup and a small piece of bread. After drinking soup, many women suffered from diarrhea. Often unable to reach the toilet in time, they squatted where they were, even if they were in their cage.

"The bread and watery soup the prisoners received was in every respect inadequate. Many prisoners died of starvation. Yet worse than the lean meals was the hazardous water supply that not only looked polluted but also tasted foul and caused all sorts of diseases." (*Seweryna Szmaglewska, Rook Boven Birkenau*)

Behind her barracks near the barbed wire Sonja finds a place where she can relieve herself. She isn't eating much so she doesn't need to go a lot. She pulls her pants up without wiping herself. Every so often she removes a thick crust of feces. Her period has stopped; some prisoners tell her that it stopped due to a chemical substance the Germans add to the soup. Starvation and fear also disrupt the cycle.

The first time she gets a piece of bread she wants to make it last as long as possible. She takes a small bite and hides the remainder under her mattress. A few hours later, when she wants to take another bite, it's gone. Shocked, she does something she regrets for the rest of her life. She takes a piece of bread hidden under a mattress that belongs to someone else. Admitting to herself to having stolen something is a tremendous shock. She decides that the next time she will eat the whole piece. But only after she rectifies the wrong she has committed. That evening after getting soup and bread, she searches in vain for the woman whose piece of bread she has 'borrowed.'

In the male camp the men hear that a Dutch women transport has arrived from Theresienstadt. The following day a man appears in her barracks. He quickly rattles off a few names, including hers.

"Herman sends you his love."

He swiftly announces several other messages and disappears. She is reassured to have heard from Herman. At the same time she feels overwhelmed by fear. When am I going to see him?

Roll call was at three thirty a.m. every morning. They were woken up to the sound of shrill whistles and yelling voices. "Get up! Get up!" The barracks leader hollered inside. "Roll call! Roll call!" Voices bellowed outside. There were thin women and super thin women. During roll call you did not want to stand next to someone who packed even the tiniest bit more weight or seemed the slightest bit healthier. Looking thinner or sicklier than the woman next to you increased your chances of standing out as "useless." The "useless" were separated from the pack and taken in the heart of darkness to the gas chambers. For fear of getting thrashed, kicked or beaten, the outside rows were also avoided.

As soon as they hear the sounds of shrill whistles, she and Sere climb down the bunk (they sleep in their rags) and run out of the barracks into the November freezing weather of 20 degrees Fahrenheit below zero. It doesn't take her long to realize that the best spot during roll call is next to somebody thinner than herself. Knee deep in the snow, in rows of ten, they line up and wait to be counted. Talking is prohibited. They know to stand deadly still. Female SS guards with whips and growling dogs move through the rows, lashing out at anyone making a sound or shifting the slightest bit. Exactly one thousand women remain standing until the count matches. If the SS man is distracted during his counting, he will start over from the beginning.

Women who fainted remained lying in the snow. Lacking resistance they often froze to death. The dead bodies in the snow and those hanging against the high-voltage wires were also counted. Roll call lasted up to three or four hours. It could take as long as six if totals didn't match. Once the numbers matched, the SS man in charge blew his whistle and everyone returned to their barracks. The slower ones were beaten until they reached the barracks.

Cold to the bone, her feet and hands are hurting. In between the roll calls she lies in her cage with Sere, speculating if they should volunteer for work.

"If they ask me I will. I want to leave this place," Sere says determinedly.

Evening roll call starts at dusk around four o'clock. It often rains. Soaking wet, everyone looks colorless, cold and miserable. The sick have a hard time standing still. Coughing and sneezing are reasons for the SS man to start counting all over again. Within a week the *KaPo* asks for volunteers.

"What kind of work?"

The *KaPo* doesn't reply. Sere volunteers anyway and leaves early the following morning. With Sere gone, Sonja doesn't want to stay in her cage. Some women walk around. Some sit and talk. Others gather around the two stoves. She gets into a conversation with several German-speaking Czech women. She finds out that they arrived on the same train from Theresienstadt. They spend time talking and they get along. One of the women sticks a moist piece of wood through a little door in the stove and drops it into the fire. Sonja places her piece of bread on top of the stove among a lot of other pieces. Not for a moment does she take her eyes off of her piece.

Until now she has not dared to leave her barracks, but she is curious. She ventures out and finds the washroom. She looks at the two long rows of filthy basins with its thirty or so faucets of which about half only dripped half a drop of water. It is so filthy that she decides it's safer not to wash. Nauseous, she hurries back to her barracks. That same evening while she is talking to the Czech women, Sere returns unexpectedly. She looks white as a sheet and moves with difficulty.

"I didn't have to work. They took me to a small room with a chair and a few bottles with a tube. They took two liters of blood from me. After the second bottle I fainted. I came to in the snow. They must have thrown me out into the snow just like that. It took me at least an hour to find my way back. All these barracks look alike. I'm so cold."

She is sore over her whole body. She lies down in her cage. Later when the "soup" is distributed, Sonja makes sure Sere doesn't miss her serving.

Most horrendous were the unexpected roll calls in the middle of the night. They were most disturbing for in reality they were mini-selections in between the big selections. Half-empty gas chambers were too expensive to run and mini-selections were used to fill the gas chamber to capacity. When the KaPo stormed into the barracks and announced an unscheduled roll call, they all knew what it meant.

Notwithstanding gnawing hunger and pain caused by her defrosting hands and feet, she finally falls asleep. Then a *KaPo* enters the barracks and screams, "Get up everybody! Roll call!" Dazed and confused they are clubbed out of their cages.

"All of you! Take off your clothes! Leave them inside!"

Sonja is freezing but does as she is told.

They are ordered to line up in a brightly lit open space. She smells the smoke from the crematoria. Everyone is terrified. They know the routine. Like a traffic cop, 'Mengele' appears and steps onto a small round platform. They are ordered to run circles around him. If he notices you and points his stick at you, you are to step out of the circle and get into the back of a waiting army truck. Nobody wants to be noticed. They are naked and freezing. It's unbearable. Sonja's hands and feet after first having thawed, freeze up again. She chooses a spot next to an emaciated woman. The woman disappears quickly into the crowd. They keep running circles around 'Mengele.' Reneetje is very thin. He points at her and a few others. Nobody ever sees Reneetje again. When the truck drives away, 'Mengele' yells, *"GEMACHT!"* "Be gone with you!"

"I'll go mad if I have to stay here any longer." An hour or so later, naked and freezing, they hobble back to the barracks. They get back into their rags and suffer the pain of thawing limbs all over again.

1944

November. "A work detail is leaving the camp," a *KaPo* calls out several times.

"They need one thousand women for a work detail outside the camp. It's walking distance. Not too far."

Relieved they volunteer, Sonja, Jettie, Sere and Florrie. All they can think of is to get away from the stinking odor and the fuming chimneys. It's still dark. Sonja and Sere march in the very last row, Sonja is the last one in the outside column. It is extremely cold. She realizes she is not dressed for this, she can barely walk but staying here is out of the question. Staying here means to die. They are stopped at the gate and counted one last time. All of a sudden Sonja feels a burning crack of a whip.

"Thousand and one!" the *KaPo* barks at her.

"Back to your barracks!"

Panicked and confused, she is too petrified to move. She gets a second flogging. Terrified she turns around. All barracks look alike. She will never find it on her own. She thinks of Sere who had trouble finding her way back in daytime. Sere! Gone. There wasn't even time to say goodbye. In the darkness, she wades through the marshy ground, several times sinking to well above her ankles. She's trying to remember her way back. She knows she has to keep going. She stumbles onto a path. Is this the right way? Everything looks alike. She is scared to death of meeting a KaPo or getting caught in the continuous scanning searchlights. She is completely lost. She encourages herself. She mumbles her father's words, "Everything happens for a reason." She hears Herman's voice, "Everything is going to be fine." She passes ten or twelve barracks. At the entrance of every barracks she goes up the two steps to the entrance, opens the door and searches for a familiar face. After fifteen or sixteen barracks, she finally sees a familiar face, Saartje Stuiver.

"Thank God."

Quickly she rushes inside. She is freezing. Her thumb is throbbing

It is hurting terribly. It's been infected since Theresienstadt, but the pain is suddenly unbearable.

"I would never have survived that walk," she thinks back in her empty cage. The barracks is quiet. "Why is my thumb hurting so much?" A doctor wrapped a piece of paper around it, but it keeps on festering. She examines it and notices she has lost her thumbnail. She is too wretched to cry.

There are about thirty or forty women left, three of which are from Holland. The following day a new female transport arrives and the barracks is filled to capacity again.

About ten days later she reports for a work detail. Her group is counted, everything is in order, but there is no train available. Two days and two nights she and the nine hundred and ninety nine other women, all dressed in rags, stand motionless in the freezing weather, waiting for a train.

Train traffic was disrupted. The SS was fighting the Wehrmacht (German army) over trains. The SS needed trains to transport prisoners deeper into the Third Reich and the Wehrmacht needed trains to transport soldiers to the front. With the allied armies approaching, the Nazis wanted to undo evidence of their crimes.

Finally after forty-eight hours a train arrives. She is exhausted, but feels relieved at the same time when the flaming chimneys disappear on the horizon. She looks at the women around her. They have little or no hair on their heads. They smell horrible. They are skin and bones wrapped in filthy rags. She hasn't looked in a mirror for months. She wonders if she looks anything like them. How did I get here again? What else does the future have in store for me? When will I see Herman again, my parents, little Judie?

The train stops outside the station of the city of Breslau. A young man on the platform sees the group of filthy female prisoners. He swears at them: "Filthy Jews!" He sees Sonja sitting next to the window. Their eyes lock and he angrily spits a thick blob of saliva against her window. She understands she must look as neglected as the others. Their train isn't moving. Nobody knows what causes the delay. All they know is that they prefer sitting in the train than having to stand outside in the cold weather. After several hours a locomotive pulling a number of open railcars arrives. They are beaten out of the train and into the open cars.

It's winter and minus 22 degrees Fahrenheit. It's unrelentingly cold. The wind-chill factor makes it ten degrees colder. Not one of them is adequately dressed. She is still dressed in the same worthless thin torn summer dress with the filthy three quarter pants underneath. She has held on to the soiled jacket and she has been using the two left shoes without socks. Her hands and toes are starting to turn black from frostbite.

They shiver in the open air and huddle together. They ride through woodlands and pastures, bound northwest for concentration camp Birnbäumel, one of ninety-seven satellite camps that make up the Gross-Rosen concentration camp complex.

All over Nazi Germany prisoners were used as slave labor in the German war industry. In Gross-Rosen they were put to work for Krupp, I.G.Farben and Daimler Benz.

The Todt Organization was a semi-state owned company, managed by Fritz Todt, a German engineer who in 1932 earned his doctorate with a thesis entitled: "Faulty street engineering applied to tar and asphalt." In 1940 he was Germany's minister of armament and munitions. His organization included construction and transport companies. He used a workforce made up of civilian slaves and concentration camp prisoners. Todt's company was responsible for building bunkers, the autobahn (the German freeways) and the Atlantic Wall, the grandest coastal defense line in history. Fritz Todt died in a 1942 plain crash and architect Albert Speer succeeded him.

BIRNBÄUMEL

The train stops in a forest just outside the tiny hamlet of Birnbäumel that consists of about ten farms. She gets off the rail car. The two women next to her don't move. She takes a closer look. They have frozen to death.

As a large group of just fewer than one thousand thin, unwashed, sickly-looking women, they walk for about three quarters of a mile through knee-deep snow into the forest. They arrive at a big open deserted camp. The very first thing she notices is that there are no guard towers and no barbed wire. She sees male and female SS guards. Sonja's immediate impression is that the camp has a different feel to it than Auschwitz-Birkenau; almost more humane. There are no flames and no chimneys and the unbearable stench of burning bodies is gone. Instead of a sadistic block leader, there is a friendly Hungarian KaPo, who lives together with her family in a separate shed.

The deserted camp comprised of ten round horse stables. Each stable was made of wood and was meant to house five horses. Now one stable needed to accommodate one hundred women. Since the horses were used to standing on firm ground, the stables had no floorboards and the women slept on the frozen ground. The outside paneling stopped eight inches above the ground. For the women sleeping on the ground, this was a recipe for draft. There were a few filthy roofless snowed-under outhouses and there was no running water in the camp.

Sonja shivers when she sees a couple of women in an outhouse are washing themselves with snow. As a child she had caught pneumonia often enough. Now she thinks, "I can die from pneumonia, but no one ever died from a dirty back."

As they arrive they are immediately handed shovels and ordered to dig to fill up the eight-inch bottom opening to stop most of the draft. In each stable one hundred women share 25 straw mattresses and a few old and dirty torn horse blankets. The mattresses are placed on the frozen ground in a circle around a small stove in the middle. A few branches they find in the snow are too wet to start a fire. She is starving, but when the job is completed, it is six o'clock and time for roll call. An SS captain appears and raises his voice.

"Is there a secretary in this group?"

Maybe mother was right after all and my typing comes in handy. If I get through this I can follow a nursing…

Her thoughts are interrupted.

"Is there a secretary in this group?"

She steps forward.

"I'm a secretary, *Herr Hauptsturmführer.*"

He walks over to her.

"Show me your hands."

He sees her abscessed thumb with the missing nail.

He starts yelling furiously.

"What are you thinking, dirty rotten Jew swine!"

The first blow drives the air from her lungs. She loses her balance and falls on the ground. He's enraged and starts kicking and beating her mercilessly.

"Do you really think, dirty rotten Jew, that I will let you give me syphilis?" He continues kicking her.

When he's finally done with her, he walks away. She bleeds from her ears and mouth. Her upper teeth are dislodged. Two women help her up.

A sergeant appears with a list. He goes down the list and checks off the names as the women yell "Present." The routine takes several hours. When he is finished he looks at this miserable transport in rags, hardly dressed for summer, let alone for winter.

"It is minus 20 degrees Fahrenheit I will try to get you clothes. If I don't succeed, I will have to send you back to Auschwitz."

A deadly silence brings back the fear she has managed to free herself from. Somebody overhears the sergeant tell his assistant, "I have to get clothes for these bitches or I'll ship them back. I don't feel like burying a thousand corpses. Call Gross Rosen and tell them I need clothes."

That first night they are dismissed and sent to their stables with nothing to eat. Saartje, Sonja, Stella, Bettie and the Czech women share the same shed. More dead than alive, they finally fall asleep.

It's four o'clock in the morning. It's dark outside, 20 degrees Fahrenheit below zero. It is a brutally cold day.

"Get up! Roll call," a voice yells. "Line up outside."

"I am so cold. I'm not going to survive this," she thinks as she neatly folds the torn blanket, before placing it at the foot of the mattress she shares.

The sergeant stops counting and yells *"GEMACHT,"* which is the signal for them to grab the shovels they leave standing against the shed, and line up. She uses this instant to disappear into the stable. Timing is crucial because after roll call they line up to march into the woods. During roll call a guard counts and inspects the so-called blankets.

Inside the stable someone has lined both sides of the central aisle with barriers made of tree branches and shrubs in a pitiful attempt to keep the snow and cold air out of the stable. She shares the mattress right next to the barrier. While she is on her knees and she has her back towards the barrier, she wraps a torn blanket around her. Suddenly she hears footsteps approaching. The door swings open and a guard sticks his head in. He inspects the stable from the entrance and leaves. She knows that getting caught means big trouble. They execute for less. She wraps herself in the blanket, but she keeps shivering. Before marching off into the woods the sergeant warns them that no one is allowed to take blankets out of the stable. After getting two slices of old and moldy bread they are on their way. Sonja eats both slices immediately.

November 1944. Hitler proclaims, "He who raises the dagger or bomb against Germany, will be destroyed ruthlessly and inevitably."

It's dark out. Guarded by *Wehrmacht* men wearing thick warm sweaters beneath their long warm winter coats, they march in -22 F. degrees weather into the forest, carrying their shovels upside down against their shoulder. A female guard yells, "Left right. Left right." When their gait is synchronized she orders them to sing. It makes them look happier.

The women like Sonja's voice and she likes to sing. Singing gives her hope. Even the German guards admire her voice. As they march past a number of farms in the village of Birnbäumel, they are ordered to sing a popular Nazi song. Two German mothers with a baby in their arms and a child with a runny nose hanging on to their skirts are chatting while watching the group marching by. A few of the bigger children stop playing and start throwing stones at them, "Dirty Jew women, dirty Jew women." The two mothers laugh, encouraging them.

If a tank drove into a ditch nose first, it couldn't reverse and back out.

"Dig!" They are ordered, "Until you see water!" So they are ordered to dig anti-tank ditches, but the ground is rock hard. It makes digging next to impossible. Once they get through the upper layer, it becomes slightly easier to dig. In freezing temperatures, they dig from six in the morning to six in the evening, knee deep in the snow. From time to time she looks up and sees the warmly dressed guards talking and laughing around a warm campfire.

For Sonja it's almost too painful to hold the shovel. The same goes for the other women who are trying to work with frozen hands and feet. But no woman dares to stay behind in the camp. Everyone knows they better join the group and pretend to be digging.

The first day, it must have been about one thirty, a man and a woman on a horse-drawn cart from a nearby farm approach. They bring two big milk containers filled with food. Sonja's group gets a dish with potatoes, meat, onions, and gravy. It's been eight months since they have eaten a proper meal. When the next group gets fed, the guards notice what's going on. Cursing and swearing they run up to the couple. One of the girls in Sonja's group says, "Quick, finish your food. This isn't for us." She was right. The following day the couple appears again, but now "lunch" means sandy water with a few blades of grass. After eating they go back to digging.

Singing helped her get through the toughest moments. Somebody would start to sing, hoping she'd join in. If she felt up to it, she would. Everybody liked her voice, even the guards near the campfire. Every so often when a guard came and checked their progress, they stopped singing and pretended to dig harder.

At six o'clock they return to the camp stiff and exhausted. It's dark by then. It's time for roll call. Her hands and toes are frozen. Somebody is missing. The captain starts counting from the beginning again. She is exhausted. She faints. The women behind her keep her upright. Finally at eleven o'clock the numbers match. They get two slices of stale bread and are sent to their stables.

She sees the Hungarian *KaPo* throw out some rotten potato skins. Can she please have them? She can't believe her luck. She shares them with her stable mates. It alleviates the hunger a little.

All of them suffer some degree of frostbite. Sonja's hands and feet are black, covered with infected wounds. She doesn't want anyone to know that she can barely walk by now. Her nose is also frozen. At night, beneath the filthy blanket her body thaws and hurts hellishly. Everybody is moaning. Women die every night. By the time she finally dozes off, it is four o'clock and time for roll call again. A supply of filthy torn and soiled clothes arrives a few days later. Only those in absolute need are allowed to take something. She doesn't dare. To everybody's surprise, Stella finds her own pretty blue coat that the guards in Birkenau had taken from her. The bonnet her mother had crocheted was still in the pocket. The KaPo allows Stella to take her own coat.

During one of the endless roll calls she looks at her missing thumbnail and tells herself that, "When I see the white crescent of a new nail, I must be liberated, or I'll give up. I am done for. I can't go on like this."

She thinks of Herman, her mother, little Judie. How are they? How is poor father? She sees him in her mind, pushing a wheelbarrow in Westerbork.

"GEMACHT!"

She quickly grabs a shovel and gets in line.

While on their mattresses trying to get warm, the girls ask her to sing. She imitates a famous singer and sings until she falls asleep. On Christmas day the Hungarian *KaPo* tells her that the guards want her to sing for them. Perhaps I can get some bread for the girls and me. They want her to do it.

Nervously Sonja follows the KaPo through the thick pack of snow to the administration stable. Inside it's nice and warm. Several guards are celebrating

Christmas with food and drinks. Her stomach aches from being so hungry. All she can think of is the bread she's hoping to get.

"I'm here to sing," she tells them shyly. They tell her what song they want her to sing and circle around her. She tries to sing a few notes but she's too weak and too nervous. She starts to cry.

"I can't do it," she apologizes.

They notice her frostbitten fingers.

"Get lost, go on, get out of here before you make us sick!"

She forgets to ask for bread. Empty handed she enters the stable.

"I couldn't. I'm so sorry. I just couldn't."

The women are disappointed but understand.

"Just as well. It's not as if you really want to sing for those bastards."

Her hands and feet are decomposing. Putrid chunks of flesh are falling from her fingers. Her toes are hanging on by a few threads of skin. In order not to lose them she has to push them back into place every so often.

1944

December. Hitler: "The German leadership is determined to brave every crisis. The Third Reich will not be deterred; it will never capitulate."

She can barely walk now. Her group encourages her.

"Keep going, or you'll be sent back to Auschwitz and you know what that means."

Then the moment they have all been waiting for arrives. In the far distance they hear the sound of artillery fire. The Russians are approaching.

January 1945. Reichsführer SS Heinrich Himmler ordered, "With the enemy approaching, evacuate all concentration camps and transport the prisoners to safer camps deeper into German territory."

(Konrad Kwiet, Dwaalweg naar het einde; Bericht van de Tweede Wereld Oorlog.)

A rumor goes around that a KaPo has said that any moment now can be the end. But camps are rife with rumors and Sonja wants to hear it for herself. At night she pretends she needs to go to the toilet and she drags herself out of the stable. She meets a female guard, who sets her at ease. "Go to sleep, it's almost over."

Monday night January 22, a guard announces, "This Friday we will evacuate. Those of you who can walk must be ready to walk to Gross-Rosen. Those of you who can't walk must report to the sick bay."

Back in the stable they calculate the odds; walking three days, 35 miles a day, at 31 degrees below zero (-23 F.) through snow and ice. Her hands and her arms are black to her elbows; her feet are frozen to her calves. She can't drag herself, let alone walk. She remembers her last words to Herman: "Stay where you are." She thinks if I walk, I'll be lost after a few steps. I'm going to die either way. It might as well be a shot in the neck in the sick bay.

Anxiously Bettie grabs her arm.

"You're not going to walk are you?"

"How can I?" She shows her feet.

"Even if I wanted to I couldn't." Bettie's eyes start rolling hysterically.

"If you stay, I stay," she shrieks as she starts pulling at Sonja's arm. Sonja pulls herself free and calms Bettie down. She asks the other Dutch women what they plan on doing.

"Saartje, why don't you stay?"

Saartje had already decided.

"I'm not going to let them shoot me. No, I am going to walk."

"Do you think that you can keep up 35 miles a day for three days?"

"I'm going to try."

"You don't know where you are going to end up. Maybe you shouldn't go," Sonja insists.

"I'm going," says Saartje

Saartje left without socks and shoes. She didn't stand a chance. Only Stella survived this infamous death march. She managed to run into an empty house and hide.

They were called death marches. Similar death marches all over Germany and Poland, left thousands of dead bodies in their wake.

About sixty women remain behind, including Sonja, Bettie and the five Czech women whom Sonja has befriended. That night they sleep in the sick bay as they were ordered. Several women with frostbitten legs as black as coal moan all night long.

When they wake up on Friday morning, it's light out and very quiet. Someone opens the door and looks out.

"There's nobody here. I think the camp is deserted."

They wait an hour before several women go out to explore.

After a few minutes they come back.

"All the other stables are empty! The guards have taken all the food. We're going to explore some more."

Then they hear gunshots. Could this be the end of the war?

A few women wander to the farms. They want to find out what is going on and possibly get their hands on some warm clothes. The guards that occupied the farmhouses are also gone. Some of the women decide to remain on the farms. Others return with warm woolen sweaters and warm coats. Nobody bothers with the women who can't walk, of which Sonja is one. She can't move and stays put. If only I could get some warm clothes and some water. She is very thirsty and eyes the icicles hanging from the slanting ceiling beams. She manages to hoist herself up and to snap a couple of them off. She keeps one and gives the rest to the others. When she lies down again she pretends to have won a lollipop. A day or two later, on a Monday afternoon, the door of the sickbay opens. An enormous Russian soldier wearing a fur cap sticks his head in. When he sees the emaciated women he gets on his knees and enters on all fours.

"Gleb," he says, "we will bring you bread."

He backs out and calls his mates. Two others stick their heads in. They too promise to bring food. She is too far-gone to realize that this is the beginning of the long road back to freedom. The sound of mortars and heavy artillery in the surrounding area continues. The Russians bring food every day. She gets a little stronger. Three weeks later when her feet have improved somewhat she tries to find a warm spot to sleep. She knows she needs to be careful for there are still Germans in the area.

She drags herself to the nearest farmhouse and knocks on the door. There is no answer, but the door is open. She enters. A woman exits the kitchen carrying a delicious smelling fruitcake, straight out of the oven.

"Please, may I sleep here?"

The woman ignores her and continues walking. Without answering her, the woman enters the family room. Sonja hears the woman say in German, "There's a filthy Jew in the hallway," before the door closes.

Frightened she continues down to the next farm. A forester with a feather in his green cap and his wife allow her to stay. For the first time she sleeps in a bed. Without sheets to be sure, but on a real mattress. The situation however remains precarious. She sleeps in her rags in case she needs to flee. She wants to wash herself, but she is afraid to undress. Every morning she drags herself from the farm back to the camp. There she listens to the latest rumors and eats the food the Russians bring by every couple of days. The Russians warn her to be very careful about eating. Her body has to get reacquainted with solid foods. Like most of the women who suffer from violent diarrhea, Sonja needs to go several times an hour. Many die from dehydration.

During the day she feels safer in the camp. Before it gets dark she goes back to the farmhouse. Only twenty women in her group of one hundred are still alive. The next day, back in the camp, she tells Bettie, "There's a second bed in the room where I'm staying. If you want you can come with me." Bettie decides to go with her.

At four in the morning Sonja wakes up with an upset stomach. She needs to go badly. She uses a bucket. When she's done she wants to go outside to empty the bucket in the woods. She opens the bedroom door. At the end of the hallway, three steps up, is the kitchen. The light is on. She hears two voices whisper in German. The door creaks.

"Who's there?" One of the voices asks.

"It's nothing. There are two Jews from the camp sleeping here." She recognizes the forester's voice.

Too scared to open the door any wider, she stays still and listens.

"Don't worry. The *Führer* has developed a new weapon. Our boys will be back in a few days and finish the job. We are going to win this war." She hears them laugh. She is terrified. She is too scared to empty the bucket and too scared to go back to bed. She sits down on the floor against the door and waits for the morning. When Bettie wakes up Sonja is still on the floor.

"What are you doing on the floor?"

Sonja gets up.

"I heard two Germans say that they are going to win this war after all. I want to go back to the camp. Do you want to come?"

Bettie gets out of bed and stands in front of her.

"So you are going back to the camp?"

"I'm scared."

Sonja turns to open the door when she feels a hysterical pounding on her back.

"You are not going anywhere. You want to leave me behind."

"It's not safe here. Come with me." Sonja tries to tell her but she doesn't get the chance.

"No! You are not leaving and neither am I! We are staying right here."

Bettie continues beating her until she is out of breath and falls on the bed. Sonja opens the door and drags herself out. She keeps going until she reaches the camp. That evening her back hurts terribly. She asks someone to examine her. She is told it is black-and-blue. Sonja knows it must be from the beating.

A secretary, now pretending to be a doctor for the sake of receiving more food, cuts off frostbitten skin, fingers, toes, and even whole feet. Sonja tells this "doctor" about the Germans on the farm and that she heard them say that Hitler is going to win this war in spite of the Russians. The quasi-doctor passes the information on to the Russians, who continue to bring food every day. For the next couple of nights Sonja finds a place on a mattress in a semi-comfortable but packed stable that the guards used for sleeping. It teems with rats looking for a warm spot.

It's the middle of the night. Sonja wakes up. Something is touching her feet. Thinking it's a rat she shakes her foot and falls back asleep. Two or three times during the night she wakes up and shakes her foot, thinking she is shaking off the rats. In the morning she notices that the arm of a dead woman is touching her foot. She realizes that what she thought were rats was the woman's hand, trying to ask for help. She feels awful. The guilty feeling for not helping this woman stays with her to this very day.

Twenty-four hours later Russian trucks arrive and take them to the city of Trachenberg, which is by now under Russian control. Before they leave, Sonja tells a soldier about Bettie staying at the second farm. A few soldiers go to the farm to get her, but Bettie refuses to leave and remains behind. It is another three or four weeks before the Russians are in full control of the area.

Concentration camp Theresienstadt

DRESDEN WROCŁAW

Theresienstadt
Prague

Czecho

Slovakia

LINZ

Vienna

Hamburger Barracks, 2003

Entrance

Maagdenburg Barracks, 2003

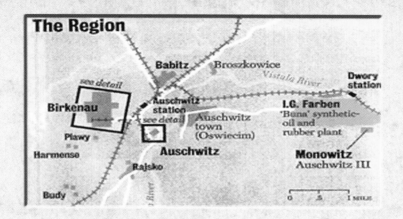

Selection at arrival

Exterior Barracks

Appel

Crosses on backs

Above: Cages inside barracks

Spoon & Fork

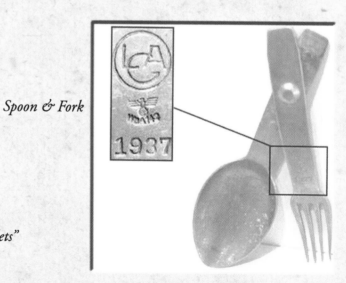

"Toilets"

Liberated

AMSTERDAM, JULY 1945

S onja leans against the inside of the front door and bursts out in tears. How can they all be gone? She gets two index-size registration cards from her purse. Her eyes are fixed on the date in red pencil, 29-6-'43 and the word DEPORTED written over her father's name. As she hangs her jacket on the coat stand, her cousin Judie approaches through the long hallway.

"Did you see my cousin?"

"Your cousin? What cousin?" She knows her cousins Aaron and Meijer are dead.

"He just left. Didn't you just see the guy in uniform leaving? That was Maurits Kiek."

Without taking a breather she continues, "He was working for the British Intelligence Service and dropped into occupied territory, captured by the Germans and sentenced to death in Belgium. The Americans finally liberated him in Czechoslovakia."

"Oh, that was Maurits? I guess I did see him."

Judie notices the cards in Sonja's hand.

"What are those?"

"My parents' registration cards. I didn't want them filed amongst the cards of the people who are confirmed dead and not coming back."

Sobbing now, she continues, "I was in such a hurry, I forgot little Judie's card."

Cousin Judie gives her a hug.

"Come on, take off your jacket. Have a cup of tea with us."

The house is remarkably empty. The few pieces of furniture in the living room are clearly second-hand, partly borrowed from a few patients, partly bought from the People's Reparation office. The house on the corner, where Jet and Anton lived before they went into hiding, has been condemned. All their personal belongings have been stolen. The whole central heating system, including the boiler and all the heaters have been ripped out. Everything made of wood has been removed and used as firewood during the cold winters of 1944 and 1945. From the ground all the way up through the third floor you can see the sky. Judie has managed to get a house assigned to her parents, so that Anton can resume his medical practice. Anton and his wife Jet have returned by way of concentration camps Vught and Bergen-Belsen.

Aunt Jet and Judie are drinking tea with Sere (the same Sere as in Birkenau) and Hennie, daughters of Jet's sisters who have not survived the war. Jet is as thin as a rake. She and Anton had been hiding with a family. The son was a policeman and felt that his father should charge Anton more money. The father disagreed and refused. The son mentioned the situation to a neighbor. The neighbor informed the police. The Gestapo arrested the father. He disappeared and was never heard from again. Anton and Jet were arrested. Daughter Judie was also betrayed and arrested. The Gestapo confronted Judie with her parents but Judie maintained through thick and thin that she did not know her parents. She convinced the Gestapo and they let her go. Anton and Jet were deported. Judie went into hiding again and became active in the resistance. Judie's brother Hans was also hiding and informed on. He too survived. Anton, Jet, Judie and Hans are one of very few families that survived the war.

Jet pours more tea and says that she visited their former neighbor. She asked him about the curtains he had offered to safe-keep. There is no denying that the velvet curtains belong to Jet and Anton. They still match the wallpaper in the room where they came from. That same neighbor also has one of Anton's paintings hanging on his wall. Jet asked him if she could please have Anton's painting back.

"That painting," the neighbor shot back, "has been hanging there for years."

"Sure," Jet answered, "but on our side of the wall."

Jet doesn't bother about the painting. She lets him keep it. There are plenty of similar stories going around. He is willing to return the curtains though. Sonja goes the following day to pick them up. The older houses have old-fashioned high ceilings and so the curtains are very long and dreadfully heavy. Carrying them is almost impossible. She puts them over her shoulders like a long veil and drags them to the new address, half a block away.

The day after she arrives back in Amsterdam, Sonja gets herself a typist's job at the People's Reparation Office, an office that keeps track of who has returned and who has not. She hasn't told anybody about her going to the Central Station every day.

"How were things at the office today?" Jet asks. Preoccupied, Sonja nods absentmindedly. While her aunt and cousins are speculating who else will return and who will not, Sonja's thoughts are with Herman. Is he coming back? His card is missing. Perhaps that means he is still alive. She bursts into tears and runs out of the room. Judie explains to the others about the registration cards Sonja brought home with her.

The bedroom has three old beds, covered with old shabby blankets. She lies down on an outside bed and bursts out crying. She lets her tears flow freely. Through her tears she notices the bunch of dried carnations on the wall, her bride's bouquet from Herman. It all seems so long ago. Her thoughts go back six months, when there was ample hope that Herman was alive...

DE DEPORTATIETRANSPORTEN
Deportation transports

15 juli	1942-1137	personen naar Auschwitz
16 juli	1942- 586	personen naar Auschwitz
21 juli	1942-1002	personen naar Auschwitz
24 juli	1942-1000	personen naar Auschwitz
27 juli	1942-1010	personen naar Auschwitz
31 juli	1942-1007	personen naar Auschwitz
3 augustus	1942-1013	personen naar Auschwitz
7 augustus	1942- 989	personen naar Auschwitz
10 augustus	1942- 547	personen naar Auschwitz
14 augustus	1942- 505	personen naar Auschwitz
17 augustus	1942- 510	personen naar Auschwitz
21 augustus	1942-1003	personen naar Auschwitz
24 augustus	1942- 551	personen naar Auschwitz
28 augustus	1942- 608	personen naar Auschwitz
31 augustus	1942- 560	personen naar Auschwitz
4 september	1942- 714	personen naar Auschwitz
7 september	1942- 930	personen naar Auschwitz
11 september	1942- 874	personen naar Auschwitz
14 september	1942- 902	personen naar Auschwitz
18 september	1942-1004	personen naar Auschwitz
21 september	1942- 713	personen naar Auschwitz
25 september	1942- 928	personen naar Auschwitz
28 september	1942- 610	personen naar Auschwitz
2 oktober	1942-1014	personen naar Auschwitz
5 oktober	1942-2012	personen naar Auschwitz
9 oktober	1942-1703	personen naar Auschwitz
12 oktober	1942-1711	personen naar Auschwitz
16 oktober	1942-1710	personen naar Auschwitz
19 oktober	1942-1327	personen naar Auschwitz
23 oktober	1942- 988	personen naar Auschwitz
26 oktober	1942- 841	personen naar Auschwitz
30 oktober	1942- 659	personen naar Auschwitz
2 november	1942- 954	personen naar Auschwitz
6 november	1942- 465	personen naar Auschwitz
10 november	1942- 758	personen naar Auschwitz
16 november	1942- 761	personen naar Auschwitz
20 november	1942- 726	personen naar Auschwitz
24 november	1942- 709	personen naar Auschwitz
30 november	1942- 826	personen naar Auschwitz
4 december	1942- 812	personen naar Auschwitz
8 december	1942- 927	personen naar Auschwitz
12 december	1942- 757	personen naar Auschwitz
11 januari	1943- 750	personen naar Auschwitz
18 januari	1943- 748	personen naar Auschwitz
23 januari	1943- 516	personen naar Auschwitz
29 januari	1943- 659	personen naar Auschwitz
2 februari	1943- 890	personen naar Auschwitz
9 februari	1943-1184	personen naar Auschwitz
16 februari	1943-1108	personen naar Auschwitz
23 februari	1943-1101	personen naar Auschwitz
2 maart	1943-1105	personen naar Sobibor
10 maart	1943-1105	personen naar Sobibor
17 maart	1943- 964	personen naar Sobibor
23 maart	1943-1250	personen naar Sobibor
30 maart	1943-1255	personen naar Sobibor
6 april	1943-2020	personen naar Sobibor
13 april	1943-1204	personen naar Sobibor
20 april	1943-1166	personen naar Sobibor
27 april	1943-1204	personen naar Sobibor
	- 196	personen naar Theresienstadt
4 mei	1943-1187	personen naar Sobibor
11 mei	1943-1446	personen naar Sobibor
18 mei	1943-2511	personen naar Sobibor
25 mei	1943-2862	personen naar Sobibor
1 juni	1943-3006	personen naar Sobibor
8 juni	1943-3017	personen naar Sobibor
29 juni	1943-2397	personen naar Sobibor
6 juli	1943-2417	personen naar Sobibor
13 juli	1943-1988	personen naar Sobibor
20 juli	1943-2209	personen naar Sobibor
24 augustus	1943-1001	personen naar Auschwitz
31 augustus	1943-1004	personen naar Auschwitz
7 september	1943- 987	personen naar Auschwitz
14 september	1943-1005	personen naar Auschwitz
	1943- 305	personen naar Theresienstadt
21 september	1943- 979	personen naar Auschwitz
19 oktober	1943-1007	personen naar Auschwitz
16 november	1943- 995	personen naar Auschwitz
11 januari	1944-1037	personen naar Bergen-Belsen
18 januari	1944- 870	personen naar Theresienstadt
25 januari	1944- 949	personen naar Auschwitz
1 februari	1944- 908	personen naar Bergen-Belsen
8 februari	1944-1015	personen naar Auschwitz
15 februari	1944- 773	personen naar Bergen-Belsen
25 februari	1944- 811	personen naar Theresienstadt
3 maart	1944- 732	personen naar Auschwitz
15 maart	1944- 210	personen naar Bergen-Belsen
23 maart	1944- 599	personen naar Auschwitz
5 april	1944- 289	personen naar Theresienstadt
	1944- 240	personen naar Auschwitz
	1944- 101	personen naar Bergen-Belsen
19 mei	1944- 453	personen naar Auschwitz
	1944- 238	personen naar Bergen-Belsen
3 juni	1944- 496	personen naar Auschwitz
31 juli	1944- 213	personen naar Theresienstadt
	1944- 178	personen naar Bergen-Belsen
3 september	1944-1019	personen naar Auschwitz
4 september	1944-2087	personen naar Theresienstadt
13 september	1944- 279	personen naar Bergen-Belsen

Single check: Jacob, Henrietta and little Judie. Double check: Sonja & Herman

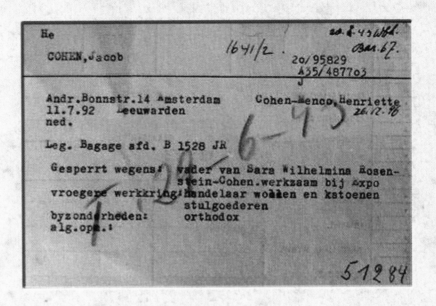

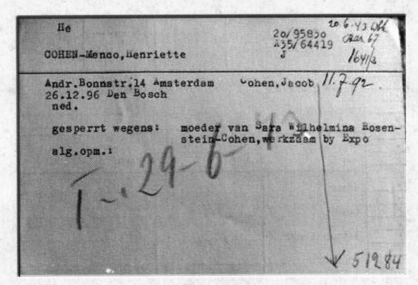

Registration cards of Sonja's parents

FEBUARY 1945

The Russians transport the survivors from Birnbäumel and the other Gross-Rosen satellite camps to the city of Trachenberg. With her five Czech friends, she finds herself in a huge building that temporarily has been transformed into a hospital. Compared to the frigid sub-zero conditions she has suffered over the previous months, the rooms are reasonably warm. She gets to eat decent food and she starts to sleep better. A friendly Russian doctor treats her hands and feet. Her body starts recuperating somewhat. For the first time since Theresienstadt, she washes herself at a sink. After four weeks of eating, sleeping and resting she is still far below her normal weight, but at least the dreadful hunger pangs are gone.

While the south of Holland had been liberated in September 1944, it would take until May 5, 1945 for the north to be free and for the war to be officially over. In spite of Holland not being accessible north of the rivers, the Russians announced that two trains would depart for the West, one through the Russian city of Odessa, the other through the city of Pilzen in Czechoslovakia. They were free but there were rumors that pogroms had started again in Poland.

This time the cattle cars are filled with layers of straw, for comfort. The cars are packed with Russian and Australian soldiers. The Russian soldiers drink themselves into a stupor, their eyes bulging out of their sockets. There are sickbay cars filled with mattresses and wounded soldiers. A Russian doctor asks Sonja to travel in a sickbay car to assist the nurses.

Although Auschwitz and its immediate surroundings had been liberated, heavy fighting continued nearby. For nearly eight weeks the train Sonja was on ran through the Carpathian Mountains, back and forth between southern Poland and Czechoslovakia.

Again Sonja tries to make sense of it all. She has a feeling her parents are not alive anymore. But Herman? Herman has to come back.

With temperatures far below zero, the Carpathian Mountains are covered with a thick layer of snow. Fighting in the area forces the train to stop constantly. During one of these stops, she goes to see her Czech friends in another car. She gets out of her car and hurries eight cars back. She can tell from their faces that something is very wrong. They tell her that during the night they were raped by several Russian soldiers. A Russian liaison officer has assigned a soldier to travel in their car with them. Sonja is speechless. The locomotive sounds its whistle. Its echoes reverberate against the mountains. The train jolts into motion. She returns to her own car. How much longer before her luck runs out? By the time she climbs into her car the train is moving.

A soldier helps her and slides the door shut behind her. By the light of the stove's fire she notices a space between two wounded soldiers. She barely sits down when she feels a hand on each thigh. She doesn't dare to look. She notices a spot near the door where she can sit. She gets up but she loses her balance. With both hands she grabs the hot duct of the stove. Her hands stick to the pipe. She screams. A few soldiers rush forward to help. She has third degree burns. A Romanian doctor dresses her wounds and changes her gauze daily.

She meets Ernie Battle, an Australian soldier. They spend weeks together on the train, going to and fro amid the chaos; Battle asks her to marry him. He wants to take her back to Australia. She bursts into tears and tells him she is hoping to see Herman again.

On April 11, 1945 the Americans liberated concentration camp Buchenwald. On April 13 the Russians liberated Vienna and on April 15 the English liberated the notorious concentration camp Bergen-Belsen. There is more good news. The Russians liberated Prague.

Displaced persons (DP's) were easily recognizable by their shabby look; by their shaven heads and by the rags they wore. Many were still dressed in their black and white pinstriped concentration camp uniforms. These DP's received free food rations from the Russians, and free of charge travel privileges.

1945

May 9. "Poland," suggests one of the Czech women, "is one huge cemetery. Why don't we leave for Prague on our own?" The others agree. Sonja decides to go with them. They take a train towards the Czech border. When they get off the train, they walk two days to the border. Her feet are killing her. She got rid of the two left shoes but walking is still very painful, because the shoes she found in the city of Lublin have no soles.

Her Czech friends tell Sonja that she should keep quiet when they cross the border. It turns out to be good advice. Once across, they continue walking. They want to get to Kosice. For weeks they hike through stunning forests and picturesque mountains. Farmers provide them with bread and allow them to sleep in their stables. The beautiful scenery is marred by evidence of the war. Even after her Auschwitz experiences, the dead bodies of a horse and its rider upset her deeply. It starts to sink in that they are free.

On a Friday evening at sundown, they meet a Jewish husband and his wife on their way to a synagogue. The couple tells them that they were hiding during the war.

"And where have you girls been?"

"Auschwitz."

"That must have been terrible. Where are you headed now?"

"We are taking Sonja to the Jewish community center in Kosice. We will continue to Prague."

"My name is Mathilde," says the woman.

"My sister Malvine Glatstein lives in Kosice."

Mathilde scribbles a note, hands it to Sonja and tells her to go and see her sister.

After a few more weeks of walking they finally arrive in Kosice. At the Jewish community center they say their tearful goodbyes.

While waiting for assistance, Sonja faints. She wakes up in a hospital. She complains that her body itches all over. They put her in a bathtub. Instantly the water turns black from dead lice. They feed her and they put her in a clean bed. Uninterrupted she sleeps for three days and nights. When she wakes up she feels a little more human again. She remembers the note for Malvine Glatstein and gives it to the nurse. Three days later Malvine and her eight-year-old son come to visit. The hospital is short of beds and after she makes a little more progress Malvine is allowed to take Sonja home to recuperate further. Malvine gives her clothes and Malvine's husband, a shoemaker by trade whose clients include the president of Czechoslovakia, provides her with a pair of shoes. They take wonderful care of her. Malvine is a great cook and Sonja gains weight rapidly. She could not have met nicer people.

The Russians announce that in cooperation with the allied countries of origin, they are preparing the journey home for all displaced persons. Displaced persons in Kosice and surroundings are mostly German, French and Belgian and a small number of Dutch survivors. They are called to report to the Russian embassy. She goes to the embassy to make inquiries.

Once at the embassy, the Russians register her as a "Displaced Person" and keep her there with thousands of other DP's.

When Malvine hears that the Russians are keeping Sonja in custody, she brings her a delicious cake. The Russians play movies showing the havoc the Nazis have created in Poland and Russia. All DP's are required to watch these movies. They see how the Nazis forced adults and children into a church, how they set the church on fire, and how the church burned to the ground with everybody in it. They see pictures of gas chambers, crematoria and lampshades made of human skin. After watching several movies, Sonja understands that her body hair, the jewelry and everything else of value that the Nazis had stolen, was sent to Germany. It starts to sink in that she might not ever see her parents and sister again. She recalls that her mother, wanting to make sure she could walk, had her feet operated on. Could they have survived Sobibor? Her dear father? And Herman? Where is Herman? Is he still alive?

A few days later she and the others are put on a train to the cities of Bielitz and Biestra in Poland's southern mountains. She knows the names of the cities because Princess Juliana and Prince Bernhard spent their honeymoon there. In Bielitz they are housed in a boarding school. Since her Czech friends were raped, she is on the alert. To prevent the Russians soldiers from knowing where she sleeps, she stays mostly in her room. She doesn't even dare to empty her bedpan in the toilet down the hall. Because of the flowerpots outside her windowsill she is unaware that her room is located above the entrance of the building. Several times she tosses the contents of the bedpan out of the window, until the one time when she hears cursing in Russian below her window. She panics and locks her door. She waits a few minutes but nothing happens.

That night a Russian soldier enters her room. She is petrified. She thinks this time she's not going to get out of it. It's her turn and he is going to have his way with her. From a room across the hall a woman's voice calls out.

"Hello! Boris, I'm over here. You are looking for me."

Boris turns and leaves the room. Again she can't believe her luck.

During her stay in Biestra she meets a few Dutch women.

"Where have you been? Have you seen so and so?"

"And you? Where have you been?"

"Is so and so still alive?"

"Do you know a Hennie Kiek?" One of the women asks her.

"Hennie Kiek? Hennie Kiek?" The name sounds familiar.

"I know that name."

The woman continues, "Hennie was in Auschwitz like you. She's always talking about her brother Maurits. He is a pilot and during the long roll calls when we saw airplanes flying over us, Hennie was always hoping that her brother was piloting one of those planes and that he would throw a rope down for her to climb up and out of Auschwitz."

Sonja understands that they are talking about Hennie, Aunt Jet's niece.

"Yes," Sonja answers, "I know Hennie. Is she alive?"

"I believe so."

Sonja feels hopeful.

A train finally departs for Pilzen, a city in western Czechoslovakia. The weather is getting better. The slow moving train is packed with grateful survivors. She often sits on the roof taking in the scenery. In Pilzen they see chickens and geese for the first time. Someone yells ecstatically, "This must be the Americans." The Russians hand them over to the Americans. The Americans give them chocolate and eggs. Then there's more good news. France has been liberated.

The Australian, English, and French governments send planes and trains to bring their nationals home. She is invited by a group of Frenchmen to join them on the train. There is one condition though. She has to stop being so childish and sleep with them.

"*Non, merci beaucoup*," she answers.

"I'll wait for a plane from Holland."

All of Holland is liberated by now. She and the rest of the small group of Dutch survivors wait in anticipation for an airplane. They wait. And wait and wait. Nobody shows up. Holland is the only country that distinguishes itself by doing nothing. No telegram, no plane, no train, no representative, not a phone call. Not a word from the Dutch government. Should she have gone back with that French group after all? She can't bear it any longer. At the beginning of June, while she is heating porridge, a Belgian government sponsored DC-3 airplane lands to pick up its nationals. (Belgium borders Holland's southern border). She and the other Dutch survivors are allowed to hitch a ride to the city of Brussels. The interior of the plane is gutted and fitted with benches along the fuselage walls. If the Belgian government had not sent an airplane, would she still be waiting? She often wonders who turned off the gas beneath the porridge.

BRUSSELS

She is free. Holland is liberated but she can't go home yet. Bus and train services have not yet resumed. Although free, she is fearful. She has a ghastly feeling that no family members are alive anymore. The Salvation Army provides her with a bed. Wandering the streets, contemplating how the rest of her life is going to play out, she runs into Bettie Caun's mother. Bettie Caun had married Jaapie Soesan, a friend of Sonja's from school. Sonja also knew Bettie's mother from Artis, the Amsterdam zoo she had visited with her father as a child. Bettie's mother has survived the war in hiding. As has become routine amongst survivors they exchange stories. Bettie's mother tells her that Bettie and Jaapie are still alive. They hug goodbye after she hands Sonja a fresh bag of cherries, the tastiest cherries ever. After they go their separate ways, Sonja breaks down and cries freely.

It's been a long time since she has encountered a familiar face, somebody tender and sympathetic towards her.

Together with one of the girls in her group she goes to a free showing of the movie "The Immortal Waltz," with Milizia Korjus. It was the same movie she had seen with her mother and little Judie in Amsterdam, before disaster had struck. She finds Brussels a bizarre experience. It almost seems as if life in this city is business as usual. The Belgians are tremendously cordial and considerate. Services like the Salvation Army, trolley services, movie theaters, later train services, are free of charge for all DP's.

It is a different story altogether at the Dutch consulate in Brussels. The Dutch consul needs a secretary. Sonja has no money and is eager to work. In a raggedy dress and an old cotton jacket that Malvine had given her months earlier, she reports to the Dutch consulate. After being hired she asks her new boss, a male secretary, for money so she can buy a pair of eyeglasses because hers were taken from her in Auschwitz.

"Are you crazy?" The male secretary yells at her. "How dare you? You have some guts asking. Go to Holland and see for yourself. Holland is a poor country. There's no money for eye glasses."

She longs to go home. Finally there's a train leaving for the city of Tilburg. She hitches a ride and continues to Den Bosch, the town where she was born only twenty-three years earlier. She visits Marietje, her mother's domestic help who had explained to her about storks and babies. Marietje still lives around the corner from the house and the huge shed with the words written on the roof: "H.S. Menco, Rags and Metals." The house and the shed are still there. It seems so long ago that she was there.

Marietje welcomes her warmly.

"Who is still alive?" Sonja asks wearily.

"They have taken everybody. All of them are dead."

Marietje's then boyfriend, by now her husband has never liked Sonja and little Judie. He feels Marietje doted on them excessively. When he comes home and sees Sonja he comments, "Well, well, you're back."

"Wouter, stop it." Marietje reproaches him, "think of everything she's endured."

"It's her own fault. They killed our lord Jesus," he shoots back scornfully.

She continues on a barge to the city of Rotterdam. From there she takes the train to Amsterdam Central Station. Her return journey may have been free of charge, but she has paid dearly.

1945

June 13. Midnight. Amsterdam Central Station. Destitute she arrives amid a large group of worn out soldiers, slave laborers and concentration camp survivors. Family members and friends are waiting for the soldiers and the slave laborers. There's yelling, crying and laughter from sheer unabashed joy.

She belongs to the bold, thin and raggedy group of zombies with unseeing eyes that move as if their souls have left their bodies a long time ago. She carries no suitcase. She owns nothing. But at long last she is back.

Nobody is waiting for her. That's okay though. She is home. She notices a table with cups of coffee and a large sign saying *FREE COFFEE*. A few in her group are dying for the taste of coffee. The station manager charges towards them.

"Hands off!" he barks, "Coffee is for workers returning from the front only."

He points to a table where Red Cross personnel are waiting for the wretched group.

"Name? Address? Where have you been?"

Indifferently the woman behind the table rattles off a list of questions. Lastly she asks matter of factly whether Sonja knows of any other survivors. She answers she has a gut feeling that her parents and her little sister have not survived Sobibor.

She glances at the clock. It's one o'clock in the morning. Everybody around her speaks Dutch. Unbelievable. She's back. Yet she can't rid herself of an ominous feeling that this isn't over yet.

The woman behind the table registers her as, "returned alive." When she is finished filling out the forms, she explains that the Portuguese Jewish hospital is being used as a shelter.

"You can go and sleep there."

"How do I get there? It is a long way from here. "

The woman looks demonstratively at her legs.

"You've got young legs. A long walk won't kill you. You should be fine. Any luggage?"

"No, no luggage. Not a dime, not a penny."

At half past one in the morning she leaves the station. With mixed feelings she starts the long walk to the shelter. At least she is in Amsterdam, far away from Auschwitz and Birnbäuml. There are no dead bodies anywhere. She is home. Yet it feels so eerie. Please God, let mother and father be alive. And little Judie and Herman. She starts hyperventilating. There's not a living soul in sight. There is rubble. Buildings are damaged, streets are broken up, and windows are boarded shut.

Of the one hundred and ten thousand husbands and wives, fathers and sons, mothers and daughters, grandfathers and grandmothers, children and grandchildren, aunts and uncles, nephews and nieces, girlfriends and boyfriends deported to "the East," one hundred and four thousand or 95 percent are dead. Murdered. The war is over. People are celebrating, but she has no feeling of freedom, no sense of joy. Holland needs to rebuild. Nobody has patience for horrible concentration camp stories.

For Sonja and her fellow survivors the misery is about to begin all over again. Who has been gassed? Who has died from disease? Who has starved to death? Does it matter? All that matters is who is returning and who is not.

Early the following morning she rings the bell at doctor Schoennmaker's, a colleague of Anton's before the war. The front door opens and there she stands eye to eye with her cousin Judie. They hug, it seems for hours.

"Nobody is coming back!" Sonja blurts out finally. She can't hold it in any longer.

"Nobody is coming back!"

"My parents are coming back. They are in quarantine. They were in Bergen-Belsen," Judie answers.

"Impossible," Sonja can't grasp how Anton and Jet could have survived the hellish concentration camp of Bergen-Belsen. However, a few weeks later they too are back in Amsterdam. They stay with doctor Schoenmaker's mother until they get a residence assigned.

When Jacob and Henrietta received their orders to report, Henrietta had given van der Linden, their non-Jewish neighbors and Mrs. Roderigues, her loyal domestic help, a number of personal belongings and valuables. For only a handful of safe-keepers it went without saying that these belongings and valuables were to be returned to the surviving owners. With the most diverse and outrageous lies, most safe-keepers refused to return the victims' personal effects. An often-used excuse was that these possessions had been a gift. And a gift was a gift.

Her knees are shaking as she rings the doorbell. Mrs. Roderigues opens the front door. She is white as a towel and looks as if she has seen a ghost. They hug and Mrs. Roderigues pulls her inside.

"Are father and mother still alive?" She whispers.

Sonja shakes her head.

"And little Judie?"

"No."

They drink a cup of tea in the kitchen. Suddenly Mrs. Roderigues bursts out and wails agonizingly. After ten minutes she dries her tears, pours another cup of tea and asks Sonja to tell her story. She sits motionless. When Sonja is finished, Mrs. Roderigues gets up. She takes a newspaper and spreads it open on the kitchen table. Next she gets a few geraniums from the windowsill. She turns the pots upside down careful to empty the soil onto the newspaper. Out of the soil appear several aspirin vials containing Henrietta's jewelry and Jacob's pocket watch. She explains that the police came by a number of times to search the house, "but they never found anything." She gets up again and this time she disappears into the bedroom. She returns with Sonja's wedding dress, silver cutlery, some of Judie's clothes, Judie's camera and a bunch of dried carnations. Finally she hands her an opened package of tea. She apologizes for having opened the package.

"There was no tea to be had anywhere," she promises, "But as soon as I get tea coupons, I'll give you a new package."

Gratefully, Sonja gives her the camera and little Judie's clothes for her two children. The neighbor who entered Sonja's parents' home after the Germans had sealed it, managed to rescue various books. He returned all of them, including "The clog maker and the Princess," She bursts out crying. She cries a lot these days. What if Herman doesn't return?

In 1942, when Jews were ordered to hand in their bicycles, Sonja and little Judie handed their bikes in to the owner of the store where Henrietta had bought them. The owner promised to safeguard them.

As soon as Sonja enters the bicycle store and the owner recognizes her, she senses something is wrong.

"I sold them, but as soon as new ones are available again, you will get two brand new bikes from me. Meanwhile," the owner suggests, "use this old bike if you like."

She looks at the old rickety bicycle. When she thinks of the horror stories of people not getting their possessions back, she thanks him and rides off in tears.

Every day, during her lunch hour and after work, she rides to Amsterdam Central Station to wait for Herman. Every day she leaves the station hoping that she may have just missed him, and that he is waiting for her at the shelter.

Leaving Central Station, for the umpteenth time she miserably grabs her bike and rides to the shelter. For the umpteenth time, she parks her bicycle. How is she going to cope with all the memories? This is the very hospital where little Judie's tonsils were taken out. Her little sister had loved the toys Aunt Betsie had hidden in her bed as a surprise after her operation and in 1942, she herself had been a patient here when they had removed her appendix.

What now? What is she to do with the rest of her life? She thinks of the letter that recently arrived from America. One of Herman's relatives has invited her.

"Come to America and start a new life."

"No," she thinks, "I am going to wait for Herman. We will go to America together."

Looking up she sees a familiar face just pulling back through an open window. She can't believe her eyes and looks again to be sure.

"Jimmy!" she screams hysterically. Jimmy's head is gone. The window slams shut. She relives the treasured last moments with Herman in Theresienstadt. Jimmy had walked ahead to the train. Herman had held her so tightly she could barely breathe.

"We'll meet again in Amsterdam."

They had kissed and kissed, and kissed again. He assured her that everything was going to be fine. She had so wanted to believe him. Then he had let go and was gone. Disappeared amid the thousands of men on their way to a similar fate.

"Jimmy!" she screams as she runs up the hospital stairs.

"Jimmy! Jimmy! You are back," she cries. Jimmy meets her in the hallway.

"Where is Herman?" she asks frantically.

Jimmy hesitates, looking for words.

"Jimmy please, I need to know. Where is Herman?" she screams.

"Sonja, Herman is dead."

She staggers. Jimmy grabs a nearby chair and sits her down.

"How did he die?"

"We were in Kaufering, a concentration camp near Dachau. We were ordered to get into a train. He was very sick, too sick to travel. He had typhoid but he absolutely insisted that we take him with us. Airplanes opened fire on our train several times. During one attack the train stopped and we were ordered out of the train and into a ditch. Herman and a few others remained in the train. When we got back, they were dead. Presumably hit by Allied aircraft fire. They had us move the dead bodies into the ditch."

She turns around, runs down the stairs, jumps on her bike and takes off. Exhausted, she arrives at the house where Mr. and Mrs. Gans are staying temporarily.

"Herman is gone. He's dead!" she screams, gutted by grief. Mrs. Gans thought of Herman as her son, even though she had been quietly hoping for years that one day Sonja would become her daughter-in-law by marrying her son Hansfried. Years later, when Mrs. Gans lay dying, both Sonja and Hansfried were at her side.

Sonja sits in the living room crying hysterically.

"He's not coming back!" she screams. Mrs. Gans tries to calm her down, but Sonja is inconsolable. She jumps up and runs out the door. She races on her bike to Anton and Jet. She bursts in and collapses. They carry her to the couch. The doorbell rings. She hears Mrs. Gans's voice.

"Is Sonja here?"

Then everything goes black. Hours later she opens her eyes. Anton is sitting at her side.

"You've cried yourself into a stupor," he tries to calm her. "When we move into our own home, you will come and live with us."

She deteriorates visibly. Until Anton and Jet move, she remains at the shelter, where Mrs. Koerts, head of Military Supervision, looks in on her. Only five years earlier, she had been in school, living with her parents, dreaming about a future with Herman. Nearly all of the teachers and children from school are dead. She is one of only a handful that survived.

She hears that the People's Reparation office is looking for personnel. She interviews and gets hired. The job is taxing. The whole day she listens to survivors' stories, sharing their ghastly accounts. Every story is different, yet similar. It is no consolation.

She holds the memories of her parents and little Judie very dear. What a great family she had come from. Mother could be strict, sometimes even angry, but that never lasted more than a minute.

In the Dutch language the word "*vroeger*," roughly translates as: "earlier" or "the past." For the Jews, it came to mean "before the war, when everybody was still alive." Sonja's life became irrevocably divided into before and after the war. Sixty-five years later, having been unable to put the past behind her, she still lives in "*vroeger*."

Nineteen forty-six was a time of new beginnings. She would marry Aunt Jet's nephew and Hennie's brother, Maurits Kiek. And although the four children they had together brought her great happiness, not much was left of that cheerful vivacious girl she had been "*vroeger*."

JANUARY 1, 2000

*N*ow in this new century, it seems as if it has never happened. As if I've never had parents. I was standing in the elevator in the Bijenkorf (a department store). Someone standing behind me said to a Jewish boy, "They must have forgotten to gas you."

"My hands are hurting, my legs feel very heavy. Only now the doctors think that I must have come back from the camps with tuberculosis."

April 10, 2001. I am visiting my mother for six weeks. Twice a year I fly from California to Holland to take care of her. We spend every minute together.

"How are you?"

"Pain, pain, pain but everyone tells me I look good."

This irritates her because it's difficult to believe that she is in such pain. The television is her loyal companion. If I even think of speaking during "The Bold and the Beautiful," I'm in big trouble. She mixes up the TV remote and the telephone. Impatiently she tries to dial on the remote and increase the TV volume with the phone.

I have come to understand that our moments together are precious. I want to spoil her as much as I know how. We went into the village and ate a pancake. She eats very little these days. Nothing tastes good anymore.

She bought a laptop and I am showing her how to send an e-mail. One day I said, "Mother, let's check your e-mail."

"I already did," she answered matter of factly, as if she's been doing it for years. She programs the VCR in no time. No blinking 12:00 in her house. She knows how to set its clock.

Today she felt so much pain; she asked me to send her friend in Israel an e-mail saying she'll mail her tomorrow. We celebrated Passover at my brother's. I cherish sitting next to my mother. From now on, I plan to celebrate every Passover with her while she is still with us.

April 11, 2001. My mother calls the bank: *"You may want to look it up in your computer."*

Quasi computer savvy she turns to me: *"They can check that in the computer, you know?"*

May 9, 2001. I'm back in Los Angeles. I'll visit her again in October. Next time I'll stay longer. I call her every day at 9 am my time, 6 pm her time, after "The Bold."

November 26, 2001. I am back in Holland. We are watching photos from *"vroeger."* She notices her fingers are still untarnished by the frostbite.

"Look, my fingers are still normal there. I remember that dark blue cardigan with those white buttons and that pleated skirt."

January 30, 2002. "Mother, how did you find out where Herman was after he was arrested?"

"Mr. Blüth often traveled to Westerbork. He told me Herman was in the barrack for criminals."

"Were you allowed to visit him?"

"I didn't. They would've kept me. I was naïve, but not that naïve.

"Did Blüth give you letters from Herman?"

"No, that wasn't allowed. He passed his messages on to me verbally."

"It's inconceivable that you had to live that way. What a difference from today. Having your own warm place."

"Yes, of course. That's something I am very grateful for. It seems very strange now. I didn't even have money to buy bread."

"Do you still think of Herman?"

"I'm carrying it with me. I don't know where he is buried. He probably ended up in a mass grave. It's impossible to grasp. In Germany more Jews were helped than in Holland. If the Nazis caught you helping Jews you were put to death. People have asked me what I would have done. I don't know that I would have been brave enough to jeopardize my family."

"The return voyage was a very difficult journey, because if not for anything else, you dreaded the future. The way we were welcomed was horrible. In the papers today, they make us sound so greedy. All we supposedly think about is money. Today, if your house is robbed, the insurance company pays you. Not so with us. We didn't even get the money the German government paid the Dutch government."

"What did your parents advise you to do when you told them you and Mr. and Mrs. Gans had been arrested?"

"They were alarmed. My mother was terrified. Everybody was."

"Were you hoping to stay in Westerbork?"

"I didn't mind having to work. There was no talk of gas chambers."

February 12, 2002. "Did you dream in the camp?"

"I don't remember."

"And now?"

"Sometimes."

"What about?"

"Father and mother. Sometimes I dream she is in the living room here. When I go to the bathroom at night I think, I imagine that mother knew I have such terrible pains."

"Hello mother, you sound tired."

"I am trying to decide if I have to take my medication now or later. I wrote it down, but I forgot. I think I took them at four o'clock. I should be taking them at five but I was late with the three o'clock one. I saw a beautiful movie, "House of the Spirits" with Meryl Streep.

"Mother, what was Herman's reaction when he arrived home the day Mr. and Mrs. Gans had gone into hiding? The day you and Mr. and Mrs. Gans were taken to the theater building and Herman arranged for you to be taken home again?"

"Mr. and Mrs. Gans wanted us to hide with them but Herman thought we didn't need to."

February 22, 2002. I call my mother every day. The routine has changed to calling thirty minutes before 'The Bold." On weekend days there is no "Bold," so we talk longer.

"Ferri, that actor friend, remember him? He told me that you seem so happy and optimistic."

"Yes, after I took my finals in high school, one of the teachers said 'we are going to miss you. When it rains you were like the sun in the classroom.'"

"Why did she say that?"

"I played the clown, made everybody laugh. We laughed a lot in those days."

"Did you like school?"

"I loved school. I loved learning."

What were your favorite subjects?"

"Music and history. I was the only one in the class who could identify notes, tones, and pitch. I always got 'A's' for history."

"Which period in history did you like best?"

"From 50 BC until 1940."

"Was your mother proud of you?"

"No, I was a bit of a handful. I took lipsticks from my mother's purse or when friends or aunts were visiting I'd open their purses and use their lipsticks."

"Why did Herman think you would be safe with Mr. Blüth?"

"Herman was in jail and I was too scared to sleep alone in the house after Mr. and Mrs. Gans had gone into hiding. After they left, Herman thought it would be safer not to stay there. Perhaps I should have stayed there."

"No, you should have gone into hiding with them."

" How could I have? Herman was in jail."

"Shouldn't you have thought of your own safety?"

"I didn't. I'm thinking if my mother had lived with all this pain I'm having, I would have insisted she'd come to live with me. Times have changed."

"You make me feel guilty."

"That's not necessary. 'The Bold' is starting. I'll call you later. "

February 2002. "Why didn't you go and live with your parents after they arrested Herman?"

"I wanted to stay near the office to get the latest information about Herman."

"Mother, I am sitting in the sun in my living room and think about how lucky I am. Do you know I was born on a Tuesday?"

"Me too. The Sunday before you were born I went to Aunt Jet. On the Monday, your father took me to the hospital and you were born the Tuesday."

"Trains left Westerbork for Auschwitz on Tuesdays. Tuesdays are my lucky days. A tarot card reader told me that if I write a book and I hand it in on a Tuesday, it would get published. How is it possible that Tuesdays are my lucky days when so many people were sent to their death on that day?"

"Mother, what about those songwriters that continued writing songs for the Germans? First they wrote for Jewish singers, then for the Germans. After the war, while in jail for collaborating with the enemy, they wrote songs again for the few Jewish singers that had survived."

"Those guys had to make a living."

Yesterday while watching the sunset I was sitting on my bench reading "Naar Eer en Geweten." (Deference and Conscience). A neighbor, originally from Argentina, joined me. She saw me read in Dutch and said she loved Amsterdam.

"This was Amsterdam," I said showing her the back cover of the book with that photo showing the field in front of the Rijksmuseum during the 1941 rally with everybody holding swastika flags.

Shocked she asked, "But that's not how it is today?"

"No, today they are in your country, in Argentina," I couldn't help answering.

"That movie I saw a few weeks ago, 'House of the Spirits,' was about that. What a beautiful movie. I have called the bookstore today. That book you asked me to get, 'From Tuesday to Tuesday' is sold out."

"Mother I booked a flight today. I'll be staying four weeks."

"Why only four weeks?"

"So I won't drive you crazy. How are you feeling?"

"Tired, but I did walk today. Walking is such an effort. My muscles don't want to cooperate anymore. My hands, my knees, my behind, everything hurts."

August 16, 2002. "What was it like waking up the very first morning in Westerbork? Did you think, "Where am I? Did you recognize where you were?"

"If I think about it now, what a crazy idea! I was relieved to be in Westerbork. I was with Herman."

"Had you seen Herman?"

"Yes and I felt I didn't have to fear being arrested anymore. My parents were there too. I wasn't scared anymore. I thought we would get through it. I had no fear. I had my parents for a week. I felt lucky to be there and not in Poland. It was tolerable. It was like a small city really."

"What was it like waking up the very first morning in Theresienstadt?"

"Herman had to sleep upstairs. In Westerbork he slept in a cabin with his uncles."

When you woke up that first morning did you go see Herman?"

"No, that wasn't allowed. Someone who had been there longer accompanied me to a place where they told me about work."

"What was it like waking up the very first morning in Auschwitz Birkenau?"

"That was a disaster. A disaster."

"What did you think?"

"I thought I was in hell. I never saw Herman again. In Theresienstadt he told me we would see each other again. I don't remember if he took his backpack. He left in a cattle car."

"Couldn't you have hidden somewhere?"

"Hidden? Where?"

"We saw a movie about that."

"Nonsense. Where would I get food?"

"Were there many women saying good-bye to their husbands like you and Herman?"

"I don't remember."

"You had no inkling that you would not see him again?"

"Of course not."

"What's the very last thing he said to you?"

"We kissed. He said in Dutch we must be strong and we will see each other again in Amsterdam."

"You actually thought you would see him again?"

"Yes. Nobody thought any different."

"Where did you think your parents and sister were?"

"When I arrived in Poland I understood that elderly people couldn't pull through. I hoped little Judie would pull through."

"She was at an age she could work."

"Yes, she was."

"What was it like waking up the very first morning in Birnbaümel?"

"That's when I started hoping again."

"Did you make friends by saying things like, 'Come and sit next to me?'"

"No, you didn't say that."

August 28, 2002. "Was your mother always home when you got home from school, as you were with me?"

"Always."

"Did she put you to bed at night?"

"When we were in bed she came to kiss us goodnight."

September 7, 2002. "How did you know that you didn't want to go to Auschwitz?"

"You didn't. Nobody knew what Auschwitz was. I asked Uncle Felix in Westerbork about the gas chambers and he said it was all propaganda. You felt something wasn't right but you didn't know what."

"I want to ask you a horrible question. The smoke that came out of the chimneys, was it black or white?"

"Gray, dark gray."

"I saw a chimney today spewing smoke, white smoke. It made me think of Auschwitz."

"It was gray. After the people were gassed they were put into the ovens. That's what you saw."

"You told me you saw the flames from the tall chimneys. But you don't see flames from tall chimneys."

"We saw flames, a big flame. When I see a chimney it always reminds me."

November 6, 2003. "Mother, did you ever see Malvine and her sister Mathilde again?"

"I wrote to them but I got no reply. When I was in Israel in 1971, I asked around and found them. He worked as a shoemaker and they had a store. I went to the store. I waited till she was done with a customer. She turned to me and recognized me. We hugged and cried. They had left for Israel a few months after I returned to Holland. That's why they had not received my letters. They were wonderful to me. Malvine's sister Mathilde stayed with us in Holland in the sixties. Her son must be in his sixties by now."

"Mother, you must have been so frightened? I am trying to imagine the reality of it all. You check your mail and you get an order that you need to pack and get ready to report at half past midnight at the Central Station. Every day when I pick up my mail I think of it. The summons states: 'Leave live household goods, i.e. pets, behind.'"

"Yes."

"You were still not suspicious of anything?"

"I thought I am young and strong. I can work. And Herman kept saying everything would be all right."

"But the guy walking you to the train, that policeman who told you not to get on that train?"

"Couldn't trust him. I just wanted to be with Herman."

"Then they force you into a cattle car. Wasn't that a sign that something was seriously wrong? Didn't you think hey wait a minute, they are not treating me right? They are crossing the line. I am not getting into that cattle car?"

"I was going to Herman."

"He had been arrested. He couldn't do anything for you."

"You don't understand."

"No mother, I don't."

November 14, 2002. "Mother, how are you?"

"Everything hurts. Pain in my hands, pain in my toes, pain in my knees and pain in my back."

"Mother, when I ask you if you believe in God, you tell me 'How can I believe in God after everything I went through?' I asked an orthodox rabbi. He said, 'Your mother surviving is God's miracle.' Don't you agree?"

"Oh, please, stop it. God is out riding his bike."

What have I learnt from my mother's story? I am asking myself now that the end of this project is in sight.

I understand why my mother did not immigrate to the United States after the war. In Holland she feels closer to her parents and Herman, just as she had felt closer to Herman in Theresienstadt in the Hamburger barracks.

I understand that due to lack of medical support, be it psychological, emotional and physical, she has never been able to overcome her trauma. When I try to grasp her answer to my continuous badgering question, "Mother, why didn't you leave?" I now understand that when you are in the midst of dire circumstances you keep shifting boundaries, you keep searching for a solution, you keep believing it's going to get better, you keep convincing yourself it's not that bad. Especially when people around you react the same way.

I now understand when I tell her to throw something or other away why she can't. Once, everything she owned was taken away from her. I understand why she can't throw out food, or why as a child, I had to finish the food on my plate. And finally I understand why she has to wave goodbye to each and every one of her visitors. Saying "goodbye" has probably been the most traumatic experience in her life.

How do I simultaneously handle my affection and aversion, my love and loathing for my mother country? I try to accept both. In the 1990's, when new information came to light emphasizing how high the actual percentage of collaborating Dutch had been, I suffered an emotional earthquake.

Dutch quislings, Dutch national socialists and Dutch SS all contributed to the fact that even in Germany the percentage of Jews betrayed, apprehended and deported was lower than in Holland. A bitter pill to swallow.

Concerning my affection, I am grateful to have been born in Holland. When the airplane I am in takes off from Amsterdam's Schiphol airport and I watch the Dutch coastline disappear beneath the clouds below, I think of the people in 1940 desperately trying to reach the shores of England. How lucky am I to be allowed to simply buy an airplane ticket, just like that. When I land in Los Angeles I am grateful for being let into the United States of America without having to navigate on all fours through a hole in the fence in the middle of the night.

Everyday is a battle to rid myself of conflict and pain. When I leave home for a short while, I hope to return a few hours later in peace and not via a detour of a couple of years.

Could something so horrendous happen again? A fact is that Jewish cemeteries and synagogues in Berlin, Düsseldorf, Paris and numerous other cities in Europe are vandalized by extreme right wing hooligans.

In Amsterdam on May 4, 2003, Holland's Memorial Day, Moroccan youngsters played soccer with a World War II memorial wreath.

When I am in a bank, the steel door to the vault reminds me of the door to a gas chamber. When running on the beach I recognize a swastika in the tire prints of the lifeguard truck. When I drive by a military shooting range, the guard tower reminds me of my mother's past.

Different people deal with pain in different ways. One starts eating, another stops eating. One becomes mad, another benevolent. I try to deal with my pain by accepting it and realizing that few people steer clear of pain. I use my mother's pain to grow, emotionally and spiritually.

I am privileged that she lives to see her memoirs completed. The journey ahead of me seems somewhat less troubled. I hope to make the best of it. One thing is sure, when I was sixteen I had to let go of my mother; with this project I have gotten her back. Unabashed joy, impossible to describe in words.

Tire tracks on the beach evoke associations.

Birkenau arrival, 1944

Birkenau arrival, 2005

Sonja, third from the left, on her yearly return to Birkenau, 1995.

"Nobody receives a program of life's concert." A reminder for all of us.

Sonja and Sinterklaas, 2004

"The Clogmaker and The Princess," Sonja's favorite book saved by a neighbor.

Peaceful demonstration when the Dutch government decides
to pardon Nazi war criminals, 1979.

May 4, Memorial Day in Holland.

Separation anxiety

Consulted sources

Beer, Regine, *KZ A5148*, Epo, Antwerpen, 1992.

Berkley, George E., *Theresienstadt*, De Kern, Baarn, 1995.

Boas, Jacob, *Boulevard des Misères*, Nijgh & Van Ditmar, Amsterdam, 1985.

Bolle, Miriam, *Dagboekbrieven*, Uitgeverij Contact, Amsterdam, 2003.

Bergh, S.van den, *Deportaties*, C.A. J. Van Dishoeck c.v, Bussum 1945.

Bloch, Werner, *Confrontatie met het noodloot*, Kamp Westerbork, 2001.

Bor, Josef, *Requiem voor Theresienstadt*, Wereldbibliotheek, 1965.

Brouwers, Jeroen, *Adolf & Eva & de Dood*, Uitgeverij De Arbeiderspers, Amsterdam, Antwerpen, 1994.

Citroen, Michal, *U wordt door niemand verwacht*, Het Spectrum, 1998

D.H. Couvee, *De meidagen van '40,* Bert Bakker/Daamen, Den Haag, 1960.

Delmar, Sefton, *De Duitsers en ik*, A.W. Bruna & Zoon, Utrecht, 1961.

Fuchs, Thomas, *A Concise Biography of Adolf Hitler*, Berkley Books, New York, 2000.

Frank, Niklas, *Vader, ik haat je*, Bertelsmann, München, 1989.

Hillesum,Etty, *In duizend zoete armen*, De Haan, Weesp, 1984.

Hillesum, Etty, *Dagboek*, Uitgeverij Balans, Amsterdam, 1992.

Höss, Rudolph, *Commandant of Auschwitz*, Phoenix Press, London, 1951.

Hondius, Dienke, *Terugkeer*, SDU uitgeverij, 's Gravenhage, 1990.

Houwaart, Dick. *Westerbork*, Omniboek, 1983.

Jong, Gerie de, *Naar eer en geweten*, Waanders uitgevers, Zwolle, 2001.

Jong, Loe de, *Het koninkrijk der Nederlanden in de Tweede Wereldoorlog*, deel 8, Den Haag, Staatsuitgeverij, 1978.

Kar, Jac., van de, *Joods verzet*, Stadsdrukkerij Amsterdam, 1981.

Kersten, Felix. *Klerk en beul*, J.M. Meulenhoff, Amsterdam, 1948.

Knoop, Hans, *De Joodsche Raad*, Elsevier, Amsterdam, 1983.

Kwiet, Konrad, *Dwaalweg naar het einde*, Bericht van de Tweede Wereldoorlog, De Geillustreerde Pers N.V en Uitgeverij Spaarnestad, Amsterdam, Aflevering 90, band 6, pagina 2514 – 2520, 1971.

Levi, Primo, *Is dit een mens*, Meulenhoff Amsterdam, 1990.

Leydesdorff, Selma, *Wij hebben als mens geleefd*, Meulenhoff, Amsterdam, 1987.

Meershoek, Guus, *Dienaren van het gezag*, Van Gennep, Amsterdam, 1999.

Liempt, Ad van, *Kopgeld, Nederlandse premiejagers op zoek naar joden*, 1943, Balans, Amsterdam, 2002.

Morse, Arthur, *Terwijl zes miljoen stierven*, Zomer & Keuning, Wageningen, 1968.

Mulder, Dirk, redactie, *Verhalen uit kamp Westerbork*, Westerbork Cahiers, 1995.

Neuman, Arthur, H.J. *Seyss-Inquart*, L.J. Veen, Utrecht/Antwerpen, 1989.

Piper, Franciszek, *Auschwitz, wie viele Juden (..) wurden umgebracht*, Universitas Krakau, 1992.

Van Pelt, R. J. en Dwork, D., *Auschwitz*, Uitgeverij Boom, 1997.

Presser, J., *Nacht der girondijnen*, Ver. ter bevordering der belangen des boekhandels, 1957.

Presser, J, *Ondergang, delen 1 en 2, Staatsuitgeverij*/Martinus Nijhoff, 1965.

Riess, Curt, *Joseph Goebbels*, Prisma boeken, Utrecht/Antwerpen, 1963.

Roegholt, Richter, *Ben Sijes, Sdu uitgeverij 's*-Gravenhage, 1988

Roper, H.R. Trevor, *The Last Days of Hitler*, MacMillan UK, 2002.

Schelvis, Jules, *Binnen de poorten*, 7e druk, De Bataafsche Leeuw, Amsterdam, 2003.

Schelvis, Jules, *Vernietigingskamp Sobibor*, 5e druk, De Bataafsche Leeuw, Amsterdam, 2004.

Speer, Albert, *Herinneringen*, In den Toren, Baarn, 1970.

Szmaglewska, Seweryna, *Rook boven Birkenau,* West-Friesland, Hoorn 1964.

Taylor, K. Kressmann, *Address Unknown*, Washington Square Press, 1966.

Velmans, Edith, *Edith's Story,* SoHo Press, New York, 1998.

Wagenaar, Aad, *Settela*, De Arbeiderspers, Amsterdam 1995.

Wielek, H., *De oorlog die Hitler won*, Amsterdamse Boek en Courantmij, Amsterdam, 1947.

Wiesenthal, Simon, *Vlucht voor het noodlot*, Becht, Haarlem, 1988.

Zee, N.van der, *Om erger te voorkomen*, Meulenhoff, Amsterdam, 1997.

Zeggelaar, J.C. van, *Vijf jaar Nazi-pers*, Excelsior, Den Haag, 1945.

Printed in the United States
78500LV00002B